Taonga Maori

*Treasures of
the New Zealand
Maori People*

An exhibition
from the collections of
the National Museum of New Zealand
Te Whare Taonga o Aotearoa

The Australian Museum

Organising Museum in New Zealand.

The National Museum of New Zealand,
Te Whare Taonga o Aotearoa

National Museum Planning and Curatorial
Committees:

Maui Pomare OBE, Museum Council Chairman
Wiremu Cooper, Assistant Director and
Exhibition Kaiwhakahaere
Janet Davidson, Ethnologist
Jack Fry, Conservation Officer
Arapata Hakiwai, Assistant Exhibition Curator
Gavin Kee, Museum Services Manager
Sir Graham Latimer KBE, Museum Council
representative
Betty McFadgen, Head of Cultural Heritage and
Exhibition Curator
Stephen O'Regan, Museum Council
representative
Warwick Wilson, Museum Information
Manager
John Yaldwyn, Director

Others involved in Exhibition preparation:

Curatorial—Ross O'Rourke, Jane Perry, Robin
Watt.
Conservation—Valerie Carson, Gina
Drummond, Shane Pasene; assisted by Jenny
Brown, Georgina Christensen, Clare Clark,
Janet Clougherty, Gaynor Duff, Felicity Roy,
Gillian Stone, Awhina Tamarapa, Sally
Thorburn.
Display—Lesley Fowler, Murray Lyndon.
Photographic processing—Eymard Bradley,
Ken Downie, Alan Marchant.
Crate design and Exhibition
coordination—Squirrel Wright. Crate
construction—Practical Studio Supplies

Organisation in Australia

Australian National Planning Committee:

Chairman: Des Griffin, Director,
Australian Museum

Rob Joyner, Chief Exhibitions
Project Manager, Australian Museum
Robert Edwards, Director,
Museum of Victoria
Alan Bartholomai, Director,
Queensland Museum
Storry Walton AM, Executive Director,
International Cultural Corporation of Australia

Exhibition Management

Organising Museum in Australia
The Australian Museum

Chairman of the Trust:
Robyn Williams AM
Director: Des Griffin

Indemnity

The New South Wales Government through
the Treasury Insurance Fund.

Australian Itinerary

Australian Museum, Sydney
Museum of Victoria, Melbourne
Queensland Museum, Brisbane

The Works in the Taonga Maori exhibition are
all from the collections of the National
Museum and National Art Gallery, Wellington.
Their loan is possible through the generosity
and cooperation of Maori tribal authorities
throughout New Zealand, the Council of the
National Museum of New Zealand and the
Board of Trustees of the National Art Gallery,
Museum and War Memorial, Wellington.

Executive Editor:
Fiona Doig

Scientific Editor:
Janet Davidson

Text:
Wiremu Cooper, Janet Davidson, Arapata
Hakiwai, Betty McFadgen, Shane Pasene,
Erenora Puketapu-Hetet

Production Coordinator:
Jennifer Saunders

Director of Photography:
Warwick Wilson

Photography:
Jan Nauta, Mark Strange

Art Direction:
Watch This! Design Sydney

Typesetting:
Excel Imaging Pty Ltd, Sydney

Printing
C & C Offset Printing Co Ltd
Hong Kong

Published by the Australian Museum, 6-8
College Street, Sydney, New South Wales,
Australia 2000.

National Library of Australia
Cataloguing-in-Publication entry:

ISBN 0 7305 6206 9
1. National Museum of New Zealand—Exhibitions.
2. Art, Maori—Exhibitions. 3. Maoris—Antiquities—
Exhibitions. 4. Maoris—Wood-carving—Exhibitions.
I. Australian Museum. II. International Cultural
Corporation of Australia.
709.01'1'099310740994

Principal Sponsor

Official International Carrier

Cover: **Figure 1. Koruru,** *gable mask,
Tūhoe tribe. (92).*

Contents   Ngā Rārangi Kōrero

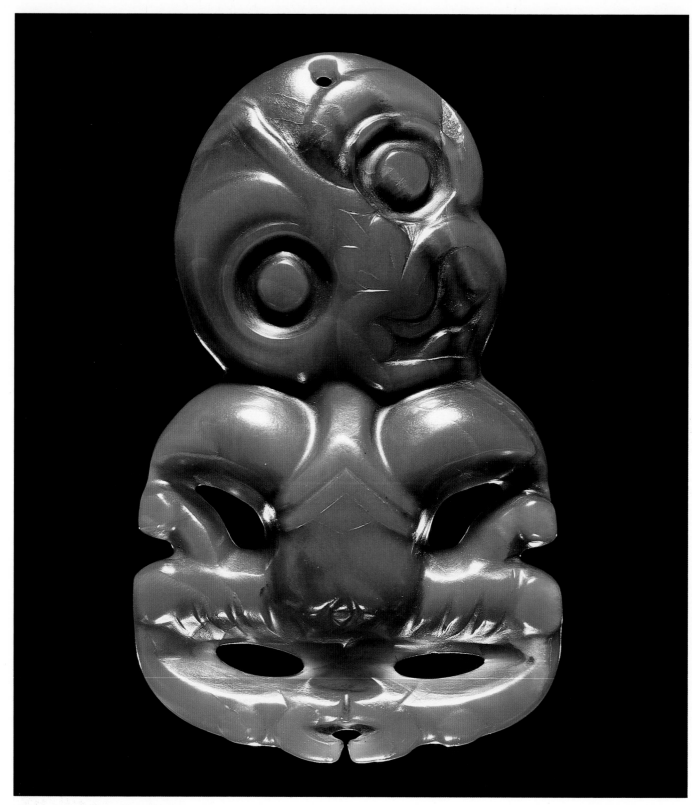

Figure 3. *Hei tiki*, neck pendant.
Made of precious *pounamu* (greenstone), the *hei
tiki* became an heirloom, gaining *mana* (prestige)
as it was handed down through the generations.
(20)

Message   He Matakupu

GOVERNMENT HOUSE

The *Te Maori* exhibition of 1983–87 showed the art and artistry of the Maori to America and to a New Zealand which was only dimly aware of its significance.

Many people feared that the culture would be trivialised and *Te Maori* would end up being a fashionable exhibition for fashionable people.

But, in a profound way, the intrinsic power and force which was in the carving or the artefact won through and silenced the viewer. People, literally, came face to face with expressions of human experience weathered by centuries of living in Aotearoa.

Culture pulls together past experience and present realities. Culture lives because it speaks of where we are now. So when their precious treasures are on exhibition, Maoris travel to be with them. The carving speaks to them and they speak to the carving.

Ponder over this exhibition. If you can, come back again and again. Let it speak to you and if that raises questions about you the viewer, then only you can provide the answers.

His Excellency the Most Reverend Sir Paul Reeves, GCMG, GCVO,
GOVERNOR-GENERAL OF NEW ZEALAND

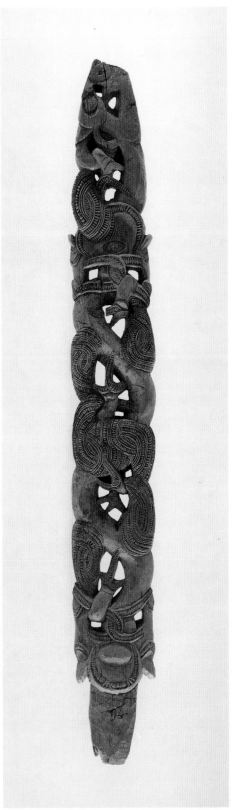

Figure 4. *Pou*, **carved post**, Te Ati Awa tribe. This unique *taonga* from Huirangi in North Taranaki is intricately carved with Taranaki-style serpentine figures. (110)

Foreword   Ngā Kupu Tuatahi

The International Cultural Corporation of Australia Limited is greatly honoured to have played a part in the tour of Australia of an exhibition of such deep spiritual and cultural power as TAONGA MAORI. We are delighted that it is the Maori people who are providing so generously this first major touring exhibition from New Zealand, and I am sure it will be a revelation to all Australians who are fortunate enough to visit it.

We are greatly indebted to the National Museum of New Zealand and its Director, Dr John Yaldwyn and to the Australian Museum and its Director, Dr Des Griffin, who together with their very capable staff have organised the exhibition. The Consul-General for New Zealand in New South Wales, Dr Richard Grant has given advice and unstinting support over two years of preparation for the event.

Such ambitious projects cannot come into existence without considerable financial support from the corporate sector, and we are deeply grateful to the companies which have generously sponsored this exhibition. We extend our gratitude also to Air New Zealand for providing transportation and ticketing assistance on a very generous scale.

This valuable exhibition has been indemnified by the Australian Government through the Department of the Arts, Sport, the Environment, Tourism and Territories, and without this vital support an exhibition like TAONGA MAORI would not be possible. We thank the officers of the Department for their expert assistance.

Above all we thank the Maori people of New Zealand who have allowed their precious taonga to make this first, long journey in Australia and we are very privileged to be entrusted with their care. It is our hope that the exhibition will inspire thousands of Australians to understand the richness and beauty of the ancient Maori culture; to appreciate its importance and strength as a living culture; and to cherish the relationship between nature and the spirit of humankind that Maori traditions so strongly express.

James B. Leslie A O MC
CHAIRMAN, INTERNATIONAL CULTURAL CORPORATION OF AUSTRALIA LIMITED

Foreword   Ngā Kupu Tuatahi

When this exhibition was first discussed with John Yaldwyn, Director of the National Museum of New Zealand, the stunning *Te Maori* exhibition had only just returned from its exciting tour of the USA. The Australian Museum's commitment to promote an understanding and appreciation of the richness and validity of diverse human cultures, meant that the visit of *Te Maori* or a similar exhibition to Australia was an enormously exciting prospect.

I am genuinely thrilled and excited that this new exhibition has been created specially for Australia. Australians will be able to see, in a way we have seldom seen before, the great significance that a people's culture has to the people — the Maori people — themselves.

This catalogue, which is the product of very fruitful co-operation between staff of the National Museum of New Zealand and of the Australian Museum, reveals to us the history and traditions of Maori people as expressed through the objects to be displayed in the exhibition.

I hope that the rich experience of viewing the exhibition of Maori *taonga* embodying the spirituality of the Maori people will be remembered by Australians for many years. It will be an opportunity in which we will be privileged to share some part of Maori culture, through the generosity of Maori people.

I congratulate all who have made this exhibition and this publication possible.

Let me close by quoting the traditional Maori proverb used in the chapter on *Te Ao Hurihuri*/The Ever-changing World:

> *He toi whakairo, he mana tangata.*
> (Where there is artistic excellence there is human dignity.)

Des Griffin
DIRECTOR, AUSTRALIAN MUSEUM

Acknowledgements   Nga Waitohu

The National Museum of New Zealand, Te Whare Taonga o Aotearoa, declares as part of its accepted policy that it will operate on the basis of a full and equal partnership between the two main cultures of New Zealand. It recognises that the *rangatiratanga*, control and community ownership, of *taonga tuku iho*, heirlooms, and *taonga whakairo*, art treasures, remains with the *whānau, hapū* or *iwi*, family, subtribe or tribe, for which the *taonga* were created.

From the bottom of my heart I wish to thank all those tribal authorities, from Taitokerau in the north to Kai Tahu in the south, for so generously giving their individual approvals for the National Museum to take their ancestral *taonga* to Australia for exhibition in 1989 and 1990. They have placed the *mana*, honour, of these works in our hands and we pass this *mana* temporarily on to Dr Des Griffin and the Australian Planning Committee to hold on our behalf while these ancestors are in their care. We are conscious of the important cultural and spiritual responsibilities this formal tribal approval carries with it, both to us at the National Museum of New Zealand and to our colleagues in Australia. With both humility and pride, the museums on both sides of the Tasman accept these responsibilities, as the currently accepted ethics and beliefs of the international *whānau*, family, of museums have prepared us both in New Zealand and Australia for such culturally sensitive roles.

I wish to thank all staff, contract workers and volunteers at the National Museum, who have worked so hard in so many ways since planning started on the Taonga Maori exhibition in 1987. Some are named in this catalogue, but many others are not mentioned here. Their invaluable help is greatly appreciated, without them all, Taonga Maori would never have been ready for exhibition in Australia on time. Planning, selection, curation, conservation, and writing for this project have all been bicultural activities, and those involved, the Museum itself, and the exhibition, have all been infinitely the better for this approach.

I wish to thank the Australian Museum Director and his staff, especially Rob Joyner, Bodo Matzick and Fiona Doig, for working so closely with us to ensure that all our cultural and spiritual requirements are met. There has been a period of learning on both sides of the Tasman and the quality and cultural sensitivity of the exhibition, as it will be seen in Australia, owe much to the ready acceptance of our needs by the Australian Museum.

Finally I would like to thank International Cultural Corporation of Australia Limited for accepting that, while the *taonga* are outside New Zealand, whether they are packed or unpacked, or whether they are on public display or not, they are treated with dignity and respect.

John Yaldwyn
DIRECTOR, NATIONAL MUSEUM OF NEW ZEALAND

He Mihi Whakawhetai   Appreciation and Thanks

E ngā waka e ngā reo e koro mā e kui mā mai te raki ki te tonga te uru ki te rāwhiti tena koutou. Tenei mātau e mihi atu nei ki a koutou katoa mō a koutou whakaaro rangatira, a koutou āwhina hoki. Ka nui te mihi mō a koutou whakaaetanga kia tukua ngā taonga kia haere ki tua ō Te Moana Tāpokopoko-a-Tāwhaki ki Ahitereiria. Kia tae tonu ki waenga ō tauiwi, ō ā koutou uri, ā koutou whanaunga me ngā kārangatanga maha e noho mai ra.

I timata ai te tikanga o enei mahi, te kimi whakaaetanga i te wā o "Te Maori". No muri iho o ngā whakaaetanga katahi ano ka tukua ngā taonga kia haere. No te whakatuwheratanga ki rawahi, ki Amerika ka rongo te ac ki te ahuatanga o te iwi Maori. Ka rongo a tauiwi ki te ihi, te wehi me te wana ō ratau mā ā ō tātau tīpuna.

Nā, kua tae te wā kā whai atu ko tenei whakaaturanga taonga Maori, i tapa ai ko "Taonga Maori". No reira e koro mā e Kui mā ko te tumanako kia mihi atu ki a ratau a koutou manaakitanga, pera i a Te Maori. Noho mai ra i roto i te ariki.

Wiremu Cooper
POU ARAHI/ASSISTANT DIRECTOR (MANAGEMENT)
TE WHARE TAONGA O AOTEAROA/NATIONAL MUSEUM OF NEW ZEALAND

This introduction outlines the history of the Maori people as it has been seen by non-Maori scholars. In the following chapters Maori people write, as only they can, about Maori mythology, culture and society, and about the meaning of the *taonga* (treasures) in this exhibition.

The Maori people are Polynesians, closely related to the inhabitants of other islands of the central and eastern Pacific. About 3,500 years ago skilled navigators with ocean-going canoes sailed into the central Pacific from the west. Those who settled in the islands of Samoa and Tonga developed features of language, culture and society which were distinctively Polynesian. These were carried by their descendants to all parts of the Polynesian triangle, which stretches from New Zealand to Hawaii and Easter Island.

Aotearoa (New Zealand) was one of the last land masses to be discovered by humans. Its long isolation had resulted in many un-usual features of plant and animal life. The only land mammals were two small bats. In the absence of animal predators, many species of flightless birds, some very large, had evolved. When the Polynesians arrived, the country was covered in forest, birds were extraordinarily abundant, and sea mammals, particularly fur seals, were very numerous around the coast.

About 1,000 years ago, the first Polynesian explorers set foot on *Aotearoa*. They were probably the first of many colonising expeditions from the region that includes the Cook and Society Islands. The Polynesians who discovered *Aotearoa* were descended from

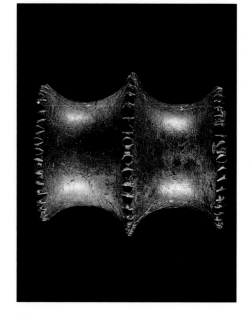

TAONG

Far Left: **Figure 5. Necklace unit,**
Ngāti Kahungunu tribal area. The first
Polynesians to reach New Zealand wore
ornaments of East Polynesian styles, different to
those of more recent times. Single stone units
such as this were sometimes handed down
through many generations as heirlooms. (42)

Left: **Figure 6. *Matau*, fishhook.**
Fishing was of foremost importance to all Maori
tribes, as it had been to their ancestors in
tropical Polynesia. (17)

A MAORI

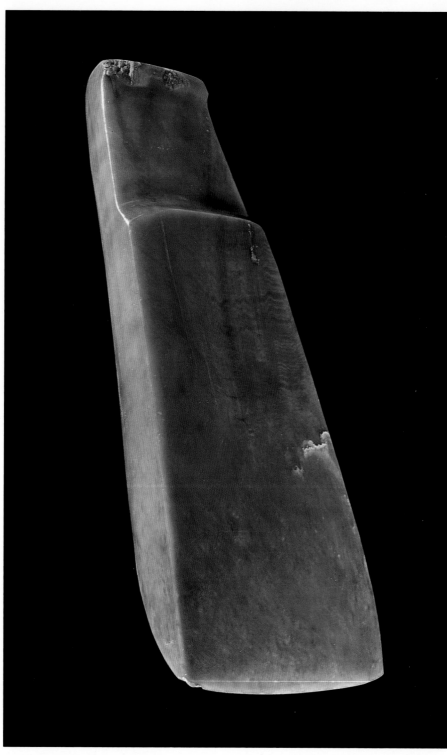

Above: **Figure 7. *Toki pounamu*, greenstone adze.** *Pounamu*, found only in remote parts of the South Island, was discovered soon after first settlement and used first for tools and later for weapons and ornaments. This adze blade is in the older, East Polynesian style. (34)

Above right: **Figure 8. *Waka*, model canoe.** Traditional Maori canoes differ greatly from the ocean-going vessels that brought the ancestors of the Maori to New Zealand. (5)

Below right: **Figure 9. *Tauihu*, war canoe prow,** Ngāti Porou tribe. The prow and stern of a *waka taua* (war canoe) are elaborately carved. (7)

people who had lived for generations on small tropical islands. They were fishermen and gardeners who took plants and animals with them on their voyages of exploration. Many of their tropical plants could not survive in temperate New Zealand, but they established several food plants in warmer parts of the country and introduced one domestic animal, the dog.

By about AD1200, the country had been thoroughly explored and there were small settlements around much of the coast. The way of life varied from region to region. The tribes in northern parts of the North Island grew a significant part of their food, although like all Maori people they also fished and hunted. Further south people gathered plant foods. They probably moved more frequently and over greater distances. However they still had villages with substantial houses where they spent the winter.

There were many changes in New Zealand during the centuries of Maori occupation. Forest was cleared, both deliberately and accidentally. Seals were driven from their northern breeding grounds by hunters. Many species of birds, including all the flightless moas, became extinct. Small fluctuations in climate made some marginal areas unsuitable for Polynesian gardening. In some regions there were significant changes in lifestyle, while in others the basis of life remained much the same.

There had always been hostilities. As population increased, however, tensions grew. About 500 years ago Maori communities began building fortified settlements, or *pā*, which became the focus of community life in many areas.

The first settlers brought with them styles of artefacts current in their home islands. Many of their small items, such as adzes, fish-

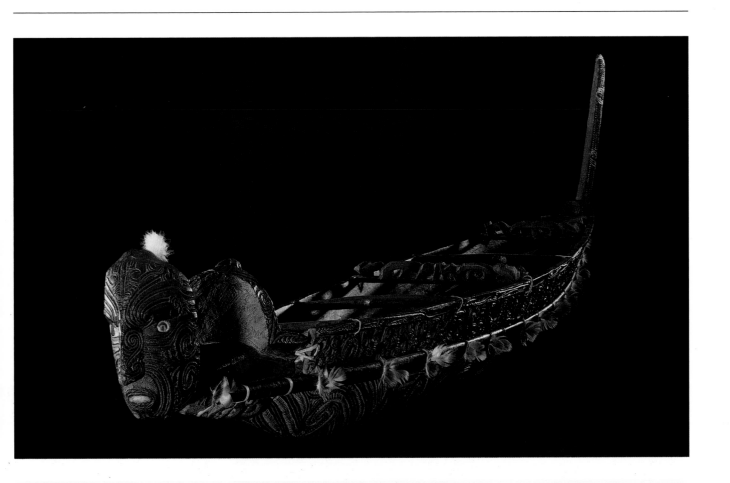

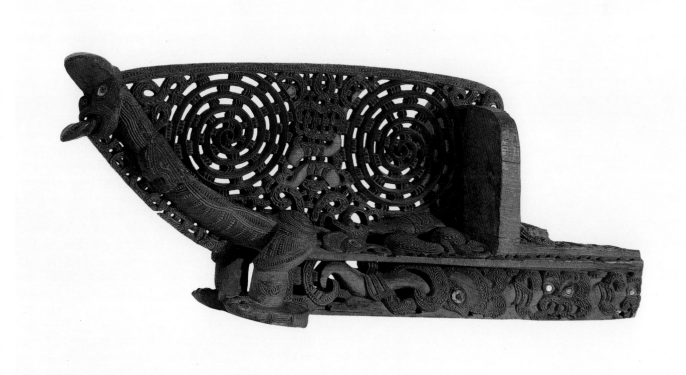

Figure 10. *Nguru*, flute. Decorative carving
has only rarely been applied to stone objects. The
wear on this *nguru* suggests it was handled and
played for many years. (50).

early efflorescence in wood carving. The value of New Zealand flax
and other plants for fibre would
quickly have been discovered
when tropical plants such as
pandanus failed. In the colder climate of New Zealand clothing was
needed for warmth as well as
adornment. Fibre was also needed
for many other purposes.

Over a period of several hundred years, eastern Polynesian
styles gave way to new and distinctively Maori styles. Some changes
were at least partly the result of
adaptation to new raw materials.
Some were changes in fashion.
Some reflected changing political
circumstances and the growth of
tribal identity. By about AD1500
most of the typically Maori
artefact styles were in existence.
Sidney Mead has described the
period from AD1500 to 1800 as *Te
Puāwaitanga* style period (the
flowering of Maori art).

Maori arts continued to grow
after the coming of the European.
There were dramatic changes,
however, paralleling the social,
economic and political upheavals
experienced by the Maori people.
Some art forms flourished while
others withered. Mead has charac-
terised the style period from 1800
to the present as *Te Huringa* (the
turning). Within it are the continu-
ation of traditional styles and the
appearance of Maori artists working in a totally non-traditional way.
Some are equally at home in traditional and non-traditional media
and contexts.

This exhibition is a celebration
of excellence in traditional Maori
art. Only a small number of the
taonga were created before AD
1500. The remainder belong to
either *Te Puāwaitanga* or *Te
Huringa* style periods. Those of
the latter period illustrate the con-
tinuation and development of traditional art. The small collection of
contemporary pieces hints at the
vitality of Maori art today.

hooks and personal ornaments,
have survived, but little is known
of their wood carving or textiles.
The need for canoes and houses
suitable for a temperate climate,
together with the abundance of
relatively soft timber and hard
stone for tools, may have led to an

Figure 11. Pendant. Kai Tahu tribal area. Rare 'bird form' pendants made of bowenite, a soft greenstone, are found mainly in the southern South Island and are probably several hundred years old. (23)

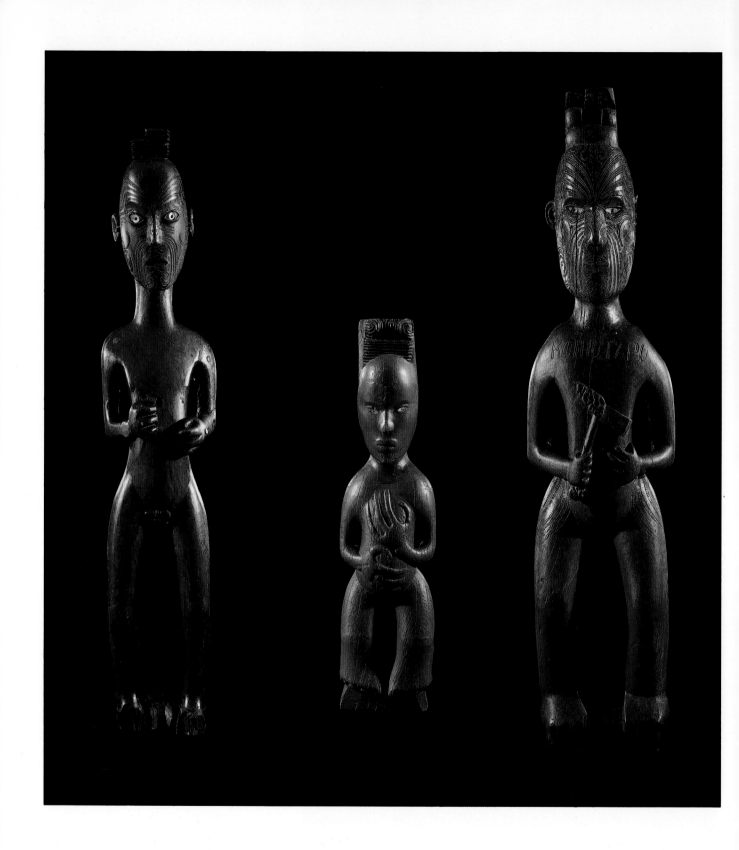

KO WAI KOIA TE

E

E kore au e ngaro

He kākano i ruia mai i Rangiātea.

I am not lost

For the seed was sown in Rangiātea.

To ask "Who are the Maori people?" is to ask about the

history and traditions, the language, customs, songs and

rituals of the Maori people. The feeling of identity and commitment to Maori things is a result of all these threads, which interrelate to form a way of life—the Maori way of life. Our traditions and myths are not just stories or fantastic events cast in the mists of time. They are meaningful and real in the sense that they validate our existence, order our chaos, and help guide our destiny.

Our *tīpuna* (ancestors) who sailed across the broad expanse of water that we call *Te Moana-nui-a-Kiwa* (The Great Sea of Kiwa: The Pacific Ocean) to this vastly different frontier known as *Aotearoa* (land of the long white cloud) are still very close to us,

helping and guiding us through this ever-changing world of ours: *Te Ao Hurihuri.*

To the Maori the past is intimately bound up with the present and future. Although our ancestors have departed into the night, we think that their *wairua* (spirit) and presence are still with us. Therefore, to answer the question "Who are the Maori people?" I must journey through time to the very creation of the world, for it is here that the Maori past, present and future begin.

In the beginning there was *Te Kore* (the nothingness, the nonexistent, the unseen). Then followed *Te Pō* (the realm of becoming, of begetting); and after

Left: **Figure 12. *Poutokomanawa*, post figures,** Ngāti Kahungunu tribe. Important ancestors are depicted on the central posts supporting the roof of a *wharenui* (meeting house). These three figures, all from different houses, are carved in the same tribal style. (2,3,4)

Below: **Figure 13. Detail of *poutokomanawa*, post figure.** The distinctive tattoo indicates that this figure is an important female ancestor. (3)

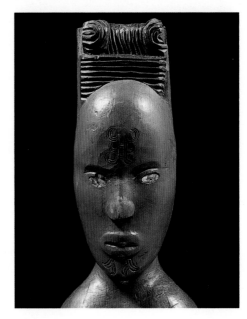

WI MĀORI?

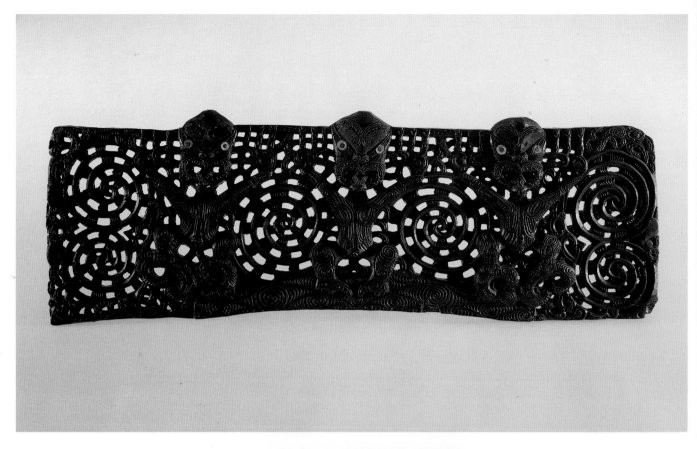

Above: **Figure 14: *Pare*, lintel,**
Ngāti Kahungunu tribal style. The carving
symbolises the separation of Ranginui and
Papatuanuku. The *takarangi* spirals between the
figures represent Te Ao Mārama, the light of day.
(99)

Right: **Figure 15. Detail of *taurapa*, war
canoe stern post,** Ngāti Toa tribe. The
takarangi spiral symbolising Te Ao Mārama is
found on both canoe and house carvings. (10)

an expanse of time there came *Te
Ao Mārama* (the realm of being, of
light and life).

For the Maori, the creation was
central to his relationships to other
kin and to the world around him:
the birds, insects, plants, fish, and
natural phenomena like the moon,
rain, mist and wind. This close and
intimate relationship with all things
was expressed in what we call
whakapapa (genealogy).

Many Maori tribes of New
Zealand had their own version of
the creation. These were learnt in
the many forms of *waiata* (songs)
and *kōrero* (talk) that were passed
down from generation to generation. All were beautiful, meaningful and unique to the tribe to which
they belonged. In the chiefly words
of this *waiata oriori* (tribal birth-
song/lullaby) of the *Ngāti Kahungunu* tribe:

> *Nō runga tāua, e, nō te
> tāhu nui atua,*

*Nō Te Kimihanga tāua, nō
Te Rangahautanga,
Nō Te Kore·te·whiwhia, nō
Te·Kore·te·rawea;
Pupuru mau ake ki te kanoi
o te uha,
Te Kā·witiwiti, e, Te Kā·
toatoa, Tira·wai·he·kura,
I hapua he tāne, Ko
Hawa·iki.*
(We are from above, from
the gods in the zenith,
We are from the searching,
from the seeking,
From the intangible void,
from the shapeless void;
Once held fast and
suspended from a female
strand,
A tapered-thing, a shrunken-
thing, [immersed in] the
blended-waters-that-flow.
Thus a male was conceived
in Hawaiki.)

In the beginning there were no
gods, no earth, no sky, no sea. Out
of this desire came the two primal
parents of the Maori: *Papatuanuku* (the Earth mother) and
Ranginui (the sky father). They
embraced in the realm of night and
seventy children were born to
them, all male, who make up the
gods of the Maori. Living in dark-
ness and longing to experience the
world of light and day, the sons
decided that their parents should
be separated. However not all of
the children agreed. *Tūmātauenga*
(the god of war) wanted them
killed. *Tāne·Mahuta* (god of man
and forests and everything that
dwells therein) thought they
should be separated, with *Ranginui* going above to the sky and
Papatuanuku dwelling on the
Earth below. In turn they tried to
separate their parents. *Rongomā-
tāne* (god and father of cultivated
foods) tried, but with no success;
Tangaroa (god of the sea), followed by *Tūmātauenga* (god of
war), also tried, but to no avail. Finally *Tāne·Mahuta* (god of man

Figure 16. *Matau*, fishhook,
Kai Tahu tribe. Maui, the great hero, hauled up
the North Island of New Zealand with a fishhook
made from his grandmother's jawbone. Fishhooks
have both practical and symbolic importance. (15)

Figure 17. Detail of *hoe*, paddle, Te Ati Awa tribe. The finely carved ancestral figure, in Taranaki style, suggests the paddle belonged to a person of high rank. (12)

and forests) placed his shoulders against the ground, thrust his feet upwards, and pushed. The sinews binding his parents stretched back and forth, heaving and swaying, until finally the parents were separated and the children experienced the *ao Mārama* (the light of day). When this happened, *Tāwhiri-matea* (god and father of wind and storms), who had not agreed to the separation, went up to the sky to be with his father. His revenge for his brothers' deeds can be seen in the storms and tempests that rage in their domains.

When the separation was completed there was only one thing lacking: the *uha* (female element). Since there were no women, *Tāne* took some clay from a place known as *Kura-waka* and fashioned it into the form of a woman. Then he breathed life into the nostrils, and thus there became *Hine-ahu-one* (the Earth-formed-maiden).

Tāne and *Hine-ahu-one* had a daughter who was named *Hine-titama*. When this beautiful girl grew up she also bore daughters to *Tāne*. As time went on she was inquisitive to know who her father was and so asked *Tāne*. His reply was "Ask the posts of the house." At this she knew immediately that *Tāne* was her father. Overcome with shame she left the world of light and journeyed to the *Pō* (the night) to a place known as *Raro-henga* (the underworld). From this time she became known as *Hine-nui-te-pō* (the goddess of the night), and it is to her domain that we descend when we pass beyond the veil.

Being a Maori, therefore, is knowing who we are and where we come from. It is about our past, present and future. Our kinship ties and descent expressed through our *whakapapa* (genealogy) are what bind us to our past and to our ancestors, and where our *mana* (power), *ihi* (prestige),

wehi (fear) and *tapu* (sacredness) come from. This is our identity; without it we have no foundation, no refuge. It is expressed in the following words:

> *He mana Māori motuhake*
> *He mana tuku iho ki a*
> *tātou.*
> (Maori spirituality set apart
> A spirituality that has been
> handed down [from our ancestors] to us.)

The answer to the question "Who are the Maori people?" is about the separation of *Ranginui* and *Papatuanuku*, the two primal parents of the Maori. It is about our ancestors who navigated the perilous seas in the many tribal canoes and who safely landed on the land we call *Aotearoa*. It is about the many tribal traditions, myths and stories which provide a solid foundation on which to order our lives. It is about our language and culture—the very cornerstones for our survival as a people. Finally, it is about love and respect for our culture, our fellow man, and our environment.

He whare maihi tū ki te wa ki te paenga,

he kai nā te ahi,

He whare maihi tū ki roto ki te pā

tūwatawata he tohu nō te Rangatira.

A carved house standing in an open space is food for fire,

A carved house standing in a palisaded *pā* is the sign

of a chief.

—Taharakau, a chief of Tūranganui

Maori society, like other societies throughout the world, is made up of an intricate web of relationships. Within Maoridom there are certain divisions, structures and groups that help determine a person's position and role. Permeating and uniting these structures is a strong force, a binding force, that we call *whanaungatanga* (kinship).

Kinship is very important to the Maori because it connects us to our kin and helps clarify the world around us. No matter where a person goes he will always feel at home because of kinship ties and the *manaakitanga* (hospitality) that is an integral part of being Maori. As the late John Rangihau,

a much-respected authority of the *Tūhoe* tribe, has said: "Kinship is the warmth of being together as a family. As children we had to live together because we were in one another's pockets. We just had to learn how to be part of an extended family."

Kinship is based primarily on descent, which can be traced through either the male or the female line. Descent provides the basis for membership of *whānau* (extended family), *hapū* (subtribe) and *iwi* (tribe).

Within Maori society the people are divided into some fifty or more *iwi* (tribes). In former times tribes varied in number from a few hundred to several thousand, and

KoTE

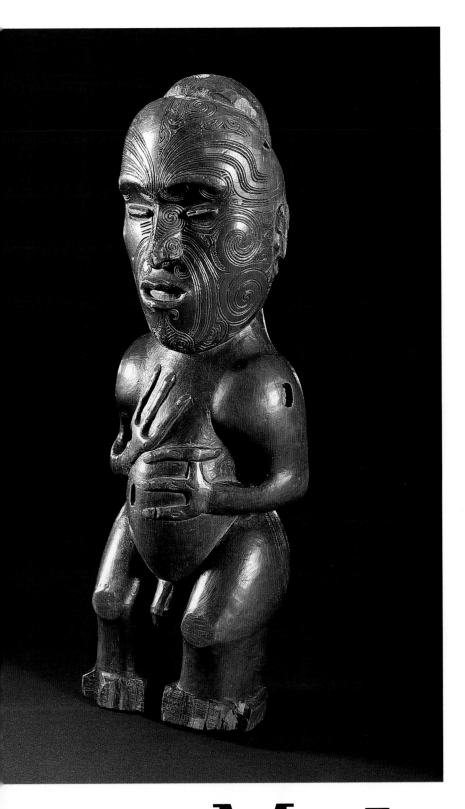

Far left: **Figure 19. Detail of *hoeroa*, chief's staff.** Weapons of whale bone, a rare and valuable material, were symbols of chiefly authority. (63)

Left: **Figure 20. *Poutokomanawa*, post figure,** Rongowhakaata tribe. This small, free-standing figure, which once had human hair attached, represents an important ancestor. It probably stood against the base of the centre post in a chief's house. (105)

WIMĀORI

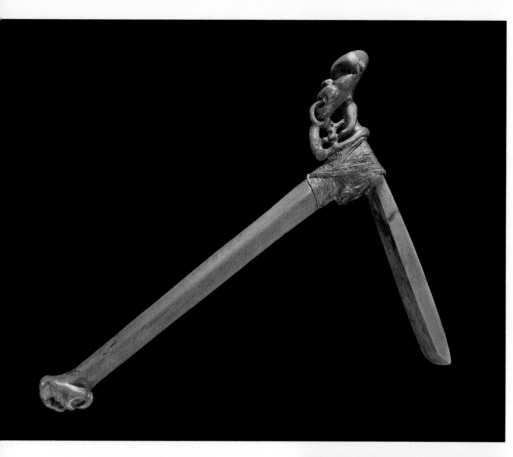

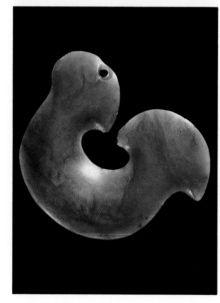

Above: **Figure 21. *Toki poutangata, ceremonial adze.*** An adze blade of *pounamu* in an elaborately carved wooden handle was a weapon and a sign of *mana* as well as a special carving tool. (75)

Right: **Figure 22. *Hei matau,* breast pendant.** A pendant of *pounamu,* in the form of a stylised fishhook, was a valuable heirloom. (29)

their territories also varied greatly in size. Political decisions were usually made and carried out by the *hapū* (subtribe) and very rarely by the tribe. Today, however, the various tribes throughout New Zealand are becoming more powerful and unified, and are a source of pride and strength to all their members.

The tribes trace descent back to the ancestors who came to *Aotearoa* in the various *waka* (canoes). These canoes are also a strong source of tribal pride. Descent may be taken from the *ariki* (chief), *tohunga* (priestly expert) or crew members. Some tribes affiliate with more than one *waka* and so the association can be a loose one.

A tribe is made up of a number of *hapū* (subtribes), each of which controls a defined stretch of tribal territory and has a considerable degree of political autonomy within the tribe. Members of a *hapū* recognise descent from a common ancestor several generations back, and take that ancestor's name for the *hapū*. For example, *Ruataupare* is the name of an ancestress of the *Ngāti Porou* tribe. Consequently the name of the subtribe is *Te Whānau-a-Ruataupare*. Since members of a *hapū* trace descent from a common ancestor, the *hapū* is a closer kin group than the *iwi*.

The members of a *hapū* operate as a group on a number of occasions, especially with regard to land matters. It is not uncommon for each *hapū* of a tribe to have its own *wharenui* (meeting house) and *wharekai* (dining hall). *Hapū* are led by *rangatira* (hereditary chieftains and leaders) who are expected to act wisely and with dignity, with the best interests of the *hapū* at heart.

A *hapū* consists of a number of *whānau* (families), which are the basic social units of Maori society. The *whānau* includes husbands and wives, children, grandchildren and great-grandchildren, and their spouses and relations. It can encompass relations from afar and is an extended family in the widest possible sense of the term. The *whānau* is under the guidance of the *kaumātua* (the respected elder of the family).

The Maori psyche revolves around tribal roots, origins and identity. Very often when we travel to other areas certain questions will be asked, such as: *Ko wai koe? No hea koe? Ko wai tō iwi? Ko wai ōu tīpuna?* (Who are you? Where are you from? What is your tribe? Who are your ancestors?). The key to these is *whakapapa* (genealogy). *Whakapapa* determines tribal identity and, in part, *mana* (prestige, power), connecting us to our *whānau, hapū* and *iwi* roots. *Whakapapa* is the essence of one's being, one's self; it links us to our past and to the *mana* of our gods; it transports us through time and provides a foundation for the present and future.

Maori society from time immemorial has relied strongly on oral traditions, by which *mātauranga* (knowledge) and *kōrero* (talk) have been passed down through the generations by word of mouth. This form of transmission permeated every aspect of tribal life. *Whaikōrero* (speech making), the many forms of *waiata* (songs), *whakapapa* (reciting of genealogies), *whare wānanga* (traditional schools of learning), *tangihanga* (funeral ceremonies), and *hui* (formal and informal gatherings) all provided opportunities for the transmission of oral traditions.

Today Maori oral tradition is still very important, although the language has suffered since the advent of Europeans and their customs, making the transmission of knowledge and *kōrero* more difficult.

Central to Maoridom is the *marae* (the meeting ground) with its associated buildings, the meeting house and dining hall. It is here

that visitors are welcomed and entertained; it is here that matters concerning the tribe or subtribe are discussed; and, most importantly, it is here that those who have passed on into the night are remembered and those who have recently departed are farewelled. It is at the *marae* that speech-making, singing, music, dancing and numerous other activities take place. The *marae* was and still is the focal point of tribal affairs. It is our *tūrangawaewae* (place to stand). Crises of life and death, light-hearted gatherings of the young, meetings to discuss tribal affairs, ceremonial speeches of welcome, *tangihanga* (funeral ceremonies) are all conducted on the *marae*. It is vibrant and alive, yet always subject to the *kawa* (etiquette and protocol) of the tribe. When the *manuhiri* (visitors)

Figure 23. *Kahu-kurī*, dog-skin cloak. The *kahu-kurī* was worn by chiefs of high rank. (137)

4172 "AWHI" ANCIENT STOREHOUSE. MAKETU.

arrive at the *marae* they know that protocol dictates that they should wait until they are called forward (*karanga*) by the *kuia* (senior women) of that *marae*.

The central building of the *marae* is the meeting house, which is usually named after an important ancestor and is also symbolically likened to his or her body. The *maihi* (bargeboards) at the front of the house are likened to the ancestor's outstretched hands; the *tāhuhu* (ridgepole) symbolises the backbone; and the *heke* (rafters) the ribs of that ancestor. In many areas the meeting house is elaborately carved and is a strong symbol of tribal pride and strength.

In former times there were *pātaka* (storehouses) close to the meeting house. These were used to store food and property for the tribe and to cater for any important event. Tribal prestige often depended on the ability to keep these *pātaka* well stocked. Today they have given way to the communal kitchen and dining hall.

Ranginui Walker, an authority of the *Whakatōhea* tribe, has summed it up beautifully when he says that the *marae* is home. It is intimately connected with the ceremonial experiences in life crises such as birth, death and marriage. To return to the *marae* from the brashness of urban life is to return to a simpler time, to a place of enduring human values.

Therefore to speak about Maori society is to speak of all these things and many more. It is about our past, our present and future. It is about the history and traditions, the lives and experiences of our forebears, of us, and of the future generations to come. We move and communicate with each other in the bonds of kinship, *aroha* (love) and respect. Our veneration for our *tīpuna* (ancestors) and their *mana* lives on with us through our language and culture. The many

marae throughout the country are visible statements of this commitment to ourselves and our culture.

Thus the following *whakataukī* (proverb) takes on a special significance within this ever-revolving world of ours:

Toi te kupu, toi te mana, toi te whenua.
The permanence of the language, prestige and land.
Without the Maori language, without the prestige and without land, *Maoritanga* will cease to exist.
—Tinirau, a *Wanganui* chief

Above left: **Figure 24. The meeting house, Tokopikowhakahau,** in 1892. The house was carved by the Ngāti Tarāwhai of Te Arawa for the Tukorehe *hapū* of Ngāti Raukawa in 1886. (103)

Below left: **Figure 25. The *pātaka* (storehouse), Te Awhi,** in 1886. Te Awhi was built at Maketu in the 1840s by the Ngāti Pikiao of Te Arawa. (83)

Figure 26. *Taiaha*, long weapon.
This *taiaha* belonged to Renata Kawepo, of the Ngāi Te Upokoiri tribe of Ngāti Kahungunu. The *taiaha* was both a fighting weapon and a symbol of authority. (59)

Right: **Figure 27.** *Waka tūpāpaku*, **burial chest,** Tai Tokerau district. This chest once stood in a communal burial cave. It is a potent reminder of the awesome power of *tapu.* (112)

Far right: **Figure 28. Detail of *Kōrere*, feeding funnel,** Tai Tokerau district. Ornate carving is a feature of these objects, which were used by men of high rank. (108)

NGĀ TIKANGA

The arrival of the first Polynesians about a thousand years ago proclaimed the arrival of New Zealand's first culture. These early settlers brought with them a rich heritage—a heritage that has its roots in mythology. The pre-European Maori, as New Zealand's first settlers became known, had no written language but relied purely on oral traditions. It was not until the arrival of the first missionaries in the early nineteenth century that a written language was adopted.

Although the Maori had no formal code of civil law as such, there was a degree of disciplinary control over the society.

This was achieved to some extent by the concept of *tapu*. *Tapu*, which is found throughout Polynesia, may be defined as "spiritual restriction" or "implied prohibition". Applied as a political medium, it was a way of making a person, place or object sacred for a period of time: rivers during the fishing season, gardens during the planting or harvesting seasons, and even forests during the bird-hunting or rat-catching season.

There were two main kinds of *tapu*, private and public. One affected individuals and the other communities. The application of *tapu* to the rivers, gardens and forest during special periods is an example of public *tapu*. It was a means of restricting access to such places so that only those experts so authorised were permitted entry. In this way, depletion of a food supply could to some extent be prevented. Sometimes *tapu* was limited to a particular object; at other times it embraced many; sometimes it was laid on one spot; at other times on an entire district.

An *ariki* (high chief) or *tohunga*

ＴUKU IHO

Above: **Figure 29. *Heru*, comb.** The head is the most *tapu* part of the body. Any object which came into contact with the head of a chief also became *tapu*. (107)

Right: **Figure 30. *Kōrere*, feeding funnel,** Tai Tokerau district. When a chief or *tohunga* was under special restriction a carved funnel was used to feed him. (108)

(priestly expert) became *tapu* as a direct result of his *mana* (status or prestige). A person could also become *tapu* by touching a dead body, coming into contact with places or objects polluted by death or private *tapu*, or by being very ill. All diseases were thought to be caused by *atua* (gods) entering the body, and these rendered the afflicted person *tapu*.

Some people and places, such as *ariki* and *tohunga* and their dwellings, were always *tapu*. Everything relating to an *ariki* was *tapu*, including his garments. These would not be worn by any one else lest that person should come to some harm. This application of *tapu* was a safeguard against possible theft. Likewise, a high-ranking chief's house was regarded as *tapu*. No person, not even the chief himself, could eat food inside it or even (in the nineteenth century) light his pipe from the hearth. A woman could not enter unless a certain *karakia* (religious incantation) was carried out.

The duration of an imposed *tapu* depended upon the person who imposed it and the reason for its imposition. The *tapu* of cemetaries and other *wāhi tapu* (places polluted by death) could be everlasting, and a special protective fence had to be built around the area or object.

Although there were other institutions such as *rāhui* and *aukati* which imposed similar prohibitions, *tapu* was by far the most important. It was so far-reaching that it entered into all aspects of Maori life. No member of the community was exempt from its stringent rules. Anyone transgressing a *tapu* committed a *hara* (violation). This demanded *utu* (payment), which nearly always took the form of disaster, whether individual or communal. In some instances violations could be overcome by seeking the assistance of a

Above: **Figure 31. Two of the eight posts,** representing the ancestors Te Rangitakaroro and Taporahitaua, in the *urupā* at Ruato at the turn of the century. (114)

Right: **Figure 32. *Poupou*, post,** Ngāti Tarāwhai tribe of Te Arawa. One of eight imposing posts that formerly stood in an *urupā* (burial ground) at Ruato, Lake Rotoiti. (114)

tohunga (priest). Where this was not possible, the *utu* process took much longer. The punishment meted out to the transgressor was inflicted not by his fellow-tribesmen but by the gods. Sometimes many years passed before the gods were appeased.

Tapu was usually beneficial, considering the society, its lack of civil law, and the fierce character of the people. It provided the basis for a controlled society. Yet sometimes it did appear to become a hindrance. It quite often restricted freedom of movement and participation in certain activities. Women, for instance, were *tapu* during menstruation and pregnancy, and therefore restricted in their activities and prohibited from entering areas such as cultivations and fishing grounds. When a high-ranking chief suffered an injury in which his blood was spilled, the spot, area or even the canoe where the accident occurred was ren-

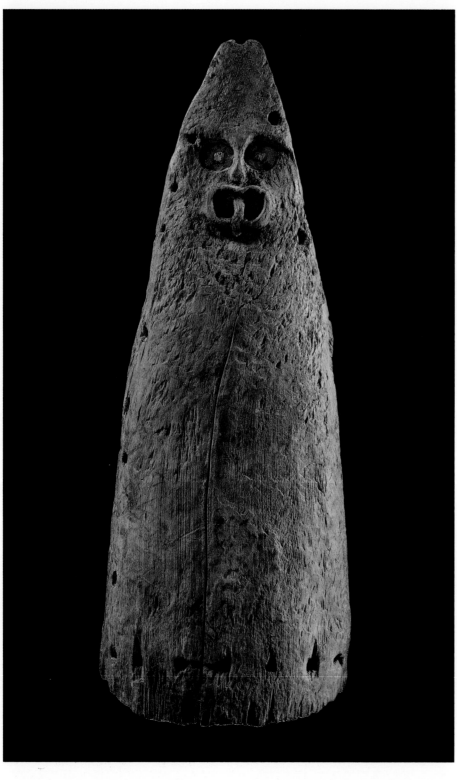

Figure 33. *Waka tūpāpaku*, part of a burial chest, Muaūpoko tribe. The end of a canoe was used to make this unique container. Canoes are associated with death rituals in many parts of Polynesia. (111)

mony of *whakanoa* (the "making common" rite). As mentioned before, *ariki* and *tohunga* were always *tapu* and could never be totally freed from the condition. Sometimes, however, they were subjected to a more stringent form of *tapu* and it was this temporary excess that the *whakanoa* rite removed. For the ordinary person, the degree of *tapu* dictated whether the ritual performed was a brief recital or a more elaborate one or, indeed, whether the *tapu* could be lifted at all.

The freeing of areas such as gardens, rivers and forests from *tapu* was a matter of acknowledging the appropriate gods—*Rongo, Tangaroa,* and *Tāne*—giving thanks for their protection, and requesting that the harvest be continuously plentiful. As a token of acknowledgment, the first fruits taken at harvest were always returned to the appropriate god as an offering.

Sometimes the *whakanoa* rite was one of purification, as in the case of burials where the bearers had been subjected to the pollution of death. Appropriate *karakia* (incantations) were invoked, which removed the pollution or cleansed them from this state.

The most common *whakanoa* ceremony regularly witnessed today is that conducted at the opening of a new meeting house. From the beginning of its construction a *tapu* is imposed. This calls on the gods to be present to provide protection during the work. Entry to the unfinished building is restricted to the men involved in its construction. When the house is completed, the *whakanoa* ceremony is performed. As well as incantations, the ceremony involves the participation of a female and the use of cooked food, for it is these elements that are the direct antithesis of *tapu*. In this way the *tapu* previously imposed is lifted and the building rendered common and safe.

dered *tapu* and therefore not useable by commoners.

It was not unreasonable, then, to expect that there would be a means of overcoming *tapu*. This was achieved through the cere-

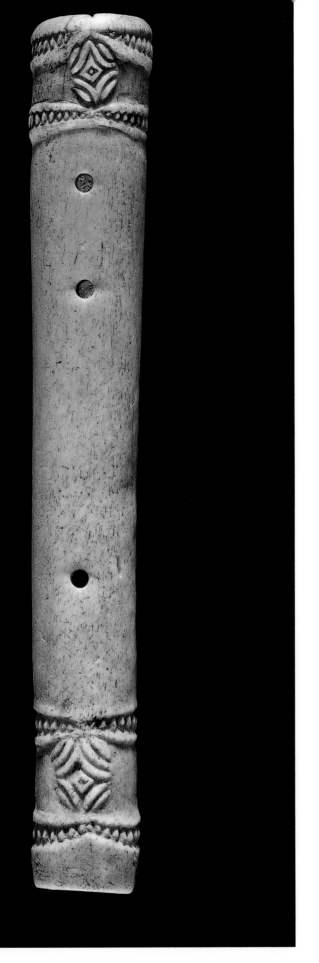

Figure 34. *Kōauau*, **flute.** Objects made of
human bone are considered to be *tapu*. (53)

He wahine, he whenua i mate ai te tangata.

Women and land are the reasons why men are lc

He kura tangata e kore e rokohanga,

He kura whenua ka rokohanga.

People die, are slain, migrate, disappear;

Not so the land, which ever remains.

These *whakataukī* (proverbs) are just two of many examples that show the relationship of the Maori to land. To speak of the land is to speak of the spiritual relationship, the union, the bond that exists between the Maori people and this precious *taonga* (prized possession) we call the *whenua*. The land is regarded as the spiritual sustenance of the Maori, as expressed in the following *whakatauki*:

Te toto o te tangata he kai
Te oranga o te tangata he
whenua.
(Food is [the source of] man's blood [bodily strength]
The land is [the source of] his well-being [his spiritual strength].)

Land was not an economic commodity to be bought and sold; it meant more—far more. It was a sacred gift from *Tāne*, a heritage passed down from the tribal ancestors, a possession that could never be sold, bartered or alienated. The close bond with the land was established long ago, at a time when the world was taking shape —when the world was still evolving.

The attachment to the land derived from the loving union of *Papatuanuku* (the Earth mother) and *Ranginui* (the sky father) and their subsequent separation by their

T E   W

Far Left: **Figure 35. Detail of *pouwhenua*, long weapon.** An intricately carved human figure decorates the shaft of this rare weapon. (64)

Left: **Figure 36. *Kūwaha pātaka*, storehouse doorway,** Ngāti Awa tribe. A finely carved storehouse was a focus of tribal pride. It held important property or prized food products such as potted birds. (85)

H E N U A

Above: **Figure 37. *Tahā*, gourd with *kete* covering,** Tai Rawhiti district. Delicacies such as birds potted in their own fat and stored in decorated containers were valuable gifts for ceremonial occasions. (81)

Right: **Figure 38. *Wahaika*, short club.** Wars were fought over land. Warriors carried both short and long weapons into battle. (68)

children. After this separation, there followed a time when the many forms of life, like the birds, insects, reptiles, fishes, and the stars and rainbows began to inhabit the kingdoms of *Papatuanuku* and *Ranginui*. Thus to understand what land means to the Maori is to know and understand the meaning of the separation of *Rangi* and *Papa*, and to realise that this act validates our existence and gives meaning to our life.

Tribal history is written over the hills and valleys, the rivers, streams and lakes, and upon the cliffs, rocks and shores. The Maori revered and respected these places

for the meaning they possessed, no matter how small or seemingly insignificant they are. The great many place names that still exist today commemorate the significance and importance of these places. In Maoridom you were brought up to know the boundary markers between tribes, the sacred places, the fishing grounds, the promontories, trees, burial places. All these places provided meaning, order and stability in an otherwise disorderly world.

Mountains are especially important to the many tribes of New Zealand. They are a recognisable symbol for their people and possess *mana* (power), strength and pride for their tribe. A mountain is more than a geographical feature; it gives the tribe meaning and stability. Thus the following *pepeha* (tribal sayings):

> *Ko Hikurangi te maunga*
> *Ko Waiapu te awa*
> *Ko Ngāti Porou te iwi*
> Hikurangi is the mountain
> Waiapu is the river
> Ngati Porou is the tribe

> *Ko Tongariro te maunga*
> *Ko Taupo te moana*
> *Ko Te Heuheu te tangata*
> Tongariro is the mountain
> Taupo is the lake/sea
> Te Heuheu is the man

The permanence of these tribal symbols is firmly entrenched in *whakatauki* (proverbs), *waiata* (song) and the *kōrero* (talk) of the tribe. Thus we have:

> *He rārangi maunga e kitea*
> *i te pō, i te ao!*
> *He rārangi tangata, ka*
> *ngaro, ka ngaro, ka ngaro!*
> (A line of hills and mountains can be seen by night and by day!
> A line of people disappears, disappears, disappears!

Figure 39. *Papahou*, treasure box,
Tai Tokerau district. The *pūwerewere* motifs on
the lid are said to be based on the patterns of
spider webs. (123)

In former times, Maori life was
dependant on the environment, on
nature. Many kinds of food and the
timber for houses, canoes and
weapons were grown and nurtured
by *Tāne-Mahuta*, the Maori god of
forests. His domain is referred to as
the *Wao-tū-nui-a-Tāne* (the great
kingdom of *Tāne*). The forests
teemed with birds, insects and
vegetation of all kinds. The Maori
took only the food and resources
necessary for their well-being, ever
mindful that any more would be
detrimental to their environment
and, more importantly, to their
gods, whose care and placation
was all important.

John Rangihau, a *kaumātua*
(elder) of the *Tūhoe* tribe, who has
since passed on into the night, has
said that everything possesses a
mauri (life force) and that the
Maori were very much aware of
the environment and how much
they owed to it. He believed, as do
all Maori people, that there is an
emotional tie to the land because
of the way Maori people have been
taught about their origins and
about the whole myth of creation.
The land is a source of strength,
dignity and *mana* (power) for the
people—it is their life-blood. To
take it away would be disastrous
for the *iwi* (tribe), *hapū* (subtribe)
or *whānau* (family). The physical
and spiritual well-being of a Maori
is linked to the land that she or he
belongs to and relates to. As
Rangimarie Pere, of the *Ngāti Kahungunu* and *Tūhoe* tribes, notes:
The land expressed Maori well-
being by right of discovery or occupation, through ancestral
inheritance, cession and conquest.

The word *whenua* is the Maori
word for the placenta, the lining of
the womb by which the foetus is
nourished during pregnancy.
Whenua is also the term used for
land, the body of *Papatuanuku*
(mother Earth), the provider of
nourishment and sustenance to
humanity. When a child was born

the placenta was buried in a special place where people would not walk over or discover it. This place became spiritual and important to that person.

The proverb at the beginning of this chapter can be translated as "Women and land are the reasons why men are lost." Adopting Rangimarie Pere's thoughts, it could also be interpreted as meaning that women and land both have the same role of providing nourishment, and without them humanity is lost.

The permanence of the land remained long after people had passed away, and the meaning, history and attachment of that land remains forever; it remains for the present generation in their lifetime, and as a source of spiritual strength and comfort for all those yet to come. What better way to conclude, therefore, than by repeating one of the most touching laments in Maori poetry. This is the farewell of *Te Rauparaha*, a famous chief of the *Ngāti Toa* tribe, to his land, *Kawhia*:

Tērā ia ngā tai o Honipaka
Ka wehe koe i au, e;
He whakamaunga atu nāku

Figure 40. *Kahu-kiwi*, kiwi feather cloak.
These cloaks were and still are highly prized possessions. The albino kiwi feathers that enhance the beauty of this cloak are exceptionally rare. (135)

Above: **Figure 41. Detail of *kumete*, wooden bowl.** Two simple but powerful figures support this wooden bowl, used for serving food. (79)

Right: **Figure 42. *Toki pounamu*, greenstone adze.** The rare and valuable *pounamu* (greenstone) is found only in remote parts of the South Island. It was made into tools, weapons and ornaments, which reached all parts of New Zealand through gift exchange. (33)

Te ao ka tākawe
Nā runga mai o Te Motu,
E tū noa mai rā koe ki au, e
Nāku ia na koe i waiho i
taku whenua iti,
Te rokohanga te taranga i
a tāua.
Ka mihi mamao au ki te iwi
rā ia,
Moe noa mai i te moenga
roa.
Ka piki e te tai; piki tū, piki
rere,
Piki takina mai rā Te
Kawau i Muriwhenua.
E kawea au e te tere,
Tēnā taku manu, he manu
ka onga noa;
Runa ki te whare, te hau o
Mātāriki.
Mā te Whare pō rutu,
Mā te Whare Ātiawa
E kautere mai rā,
Whakaurupā taku aroha,
na-i.
Oh ye waters of *Honipaka*,
From you, alas, I now depart,
But my spirit still clings
To that cloud floating
Thither from *Te Motu*,
Which remains there, my
fate unheeding.
I now sorrowfully forsake my
cherished land;
Unexpected indeed is this our
parting;
A tribute now I render to my
forsaken people,
Who lie there in their last
long sleep.
The tides will forever ebb
and flow,
Lamenting as they flow o'er
Te Kawau at *Muriwhenua*.
A fugitive in hasty flight am
I,
Leaving there, a cherished
bird forever;
Held captive within the house
and in this summer weather
Let the House of Mourning,
Let the House of *Atiawa*,
Lament and deluge with
tears
This grave of all my sorrows.

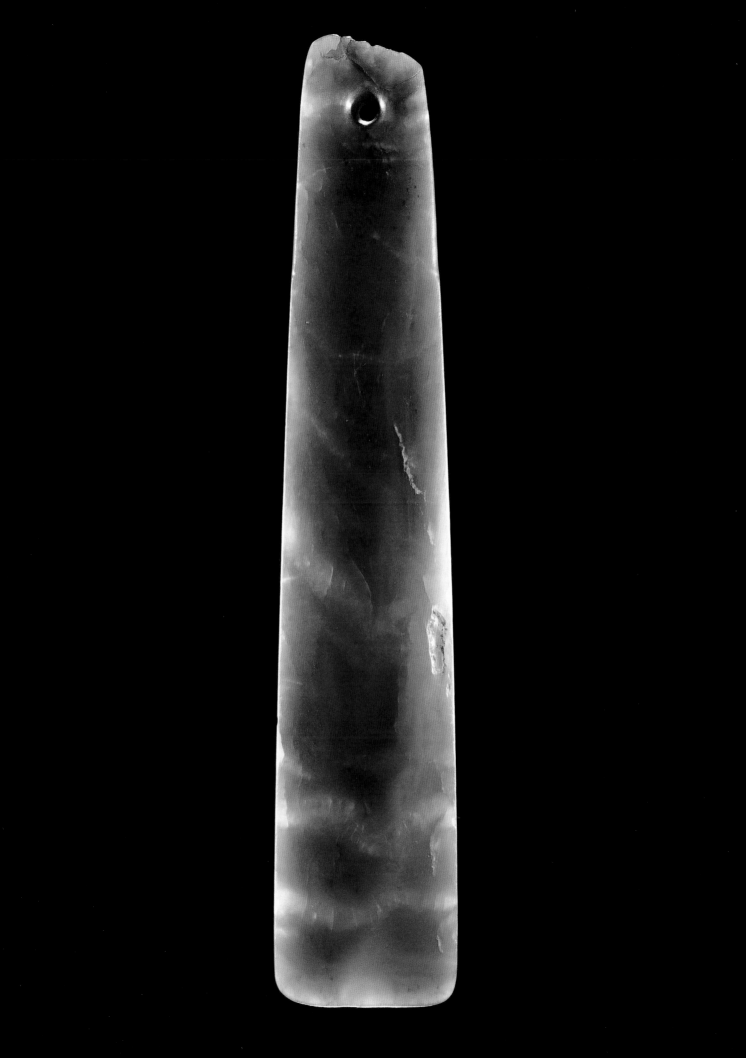

Right: **Figure 43. *Koruru*, gable mask,** Tūhoe tribe. A carved house represents the body of an ancestor, crouching over and sheltering the descendants. The *koruru*, at the apex of the house front, is seen as the ancestor's head. (92)

Far right: **Figure 44. Detail of *pūtōrino*, bugle-flute.** Small objects as well as large buildings and canoes were ornamented with carvings of ancestors and mythological figures. (44)

TE TOI WHA

Maori art reflects the total environment and the many forces that operate within it. It is an expression of the unity of all things around us. Although many people see contradictions in the world, the Maori view of the cosmos, the creation and our ancestors is coherent and unified. Through our art we see a

visible connection between past and present; a connection that provides meaning and stability for generations yet to come. Our art is a visible and strong symbol of Maori identity and pride. Our artworks invoke feelings of *ihi* (power), *wehi* (fear) and *wana* (excitement, thrill), because we believe that our art heritage is very much alive. We shed tears over our *taonga* in remembrance of our ancestors who have passed on into the night.

Sidney Mead, an authority on Maori and Pacific art, has expressed this enduring attachment well:

We treat our artwork as people because many of them represent our ancestors who for us are real persons. Though they died generations ago they live in our memories and we live with them for they are an essential part of our identity as Maori individuals. They are anchor points in our genealogies and in our history. Without them we have no position in society and we have no social reality. We form with them the social universe of Maoridom.

Our art tradition was brought to *Aotearoa* from central Polynesia and has developed locally for hundreds of years. The extent of this local development can be clearly

KAIRO

Figure 45: *Tekoteko*, **gable figure,**
Tai Rawhiti district. In one tribal account of the
origin of carving, Ruatepupuke's son Manuruhi
was turned into a carved wooden *tekoteko*. (89)

was a vehicle through whom the gods created and communicated. The carvers were seen as carrying on a much-respected and highly-valued art form—a godly art form. This view is still prevalent in Maori society today.

In former times, carving was subject to the observances of *tapu* (religious restriction) in order to appease and placate the gods whose care and protection was all-important. A carver never blew the chips away or used them to cook food. Women were not permitted near the carvings, and when tobacco was introduced smoking was not allowed while carving. If the *tapu* was transgressed there was a real fear that something would happen to exact payment. Although *tapu* is still very pervasive today, some master carvers feel that full adherence to it is difficult to enforce.

To understand the carving tradition is also to understand the history, traditions, language and religion of the Maori. All things possessed a *mauri* (life force) and *wairua* (spirit). To cut down a tree from the forest was to fell an offspring of *Tāne-Mahuta*, the god of forests and man. Before such an act was begun, therefore, certain rituals had to be performed so that things could proceed smoothly and safely. The following *karakia* (ritual incantation) was recited by the *tohunga* (priestly expert) before one of the offspring of *Tāne* was felled to the ground. Its language is archaic, but full of beauty.

seen in what we refer to as *te toi whakairo* (the art of Maori carving).

Carving was a sacred, honoured and cherished profession. *Tohunga whakairo* (master carvers) were men of distinction and fame. The Maori people shared the Polynesian belief that the artist

Kākāriki pōwhaitere
I te Wao-nui-a-Tāne
I te uranga tapu
Kua ara, kua ara
A Tāne ki runga
Kua kotia ngā pūtake
O te rākau o te whare nei;
Kua waiho atu
I te urunga tapu;
Kua kotia ngā kauru
O te rākau o te whare nei;

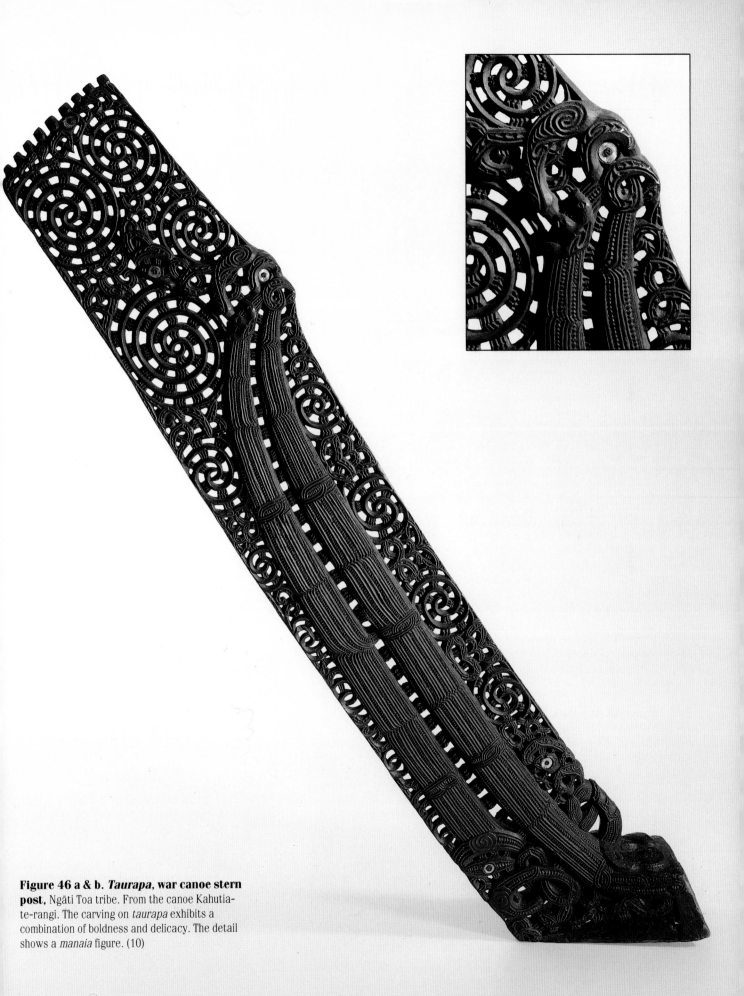

Figure 46 a & b. *Taurapa*, **war canoe stern post,** Ngāti Toa tribe. From the canoe Kahutia-te-rangi. The carving on *taurapa* exhibits a combination of boldness and delicacy. The detail shows a *manaia* figure. (10)

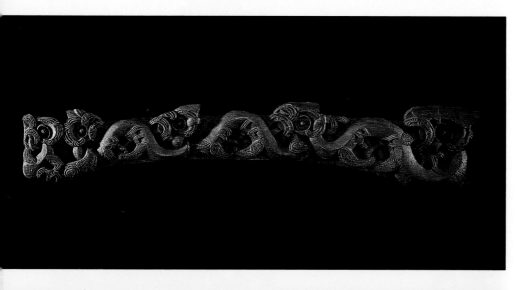

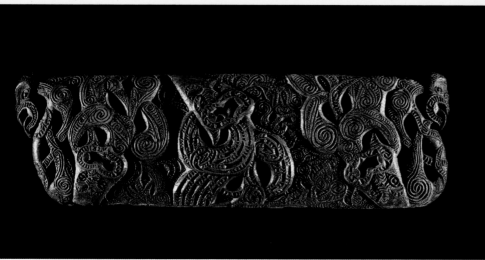

Above: **Figure 47. *Paepae*, threshold of a storehouse,** Te Ati Awa tribe. Serpentine figures and pointed heads are characteristic of the Taranaki carving style. (88)

Below: **Figure 48. *Papahou*, treasure box,** Tai Tokerau district. The typical serpentine figures and pear-shaped heads of the northern carving style are seen on this ornately carved box. (121)

*Kua waiho atu
I te Wao-nui-a Tāne
Kua tae au
Ki ngā pukenga
Ki ngā wānanga
Ki ngā tauira
Patua kuru
Patua whao
Patua te toki a Tai-haruru.
Kua piki hoki nei
Ki te maro-hukahuka-nui
A Tangaroa
Te ngaru ai e whati ai.
E Nuku-tai-maroro
Kāore ko au
E kimi ana, e hahau ana
I ngā uri o te whānau a
Rata
Hai pokapoka ia Tāne
E Tui-i-i*

*Kāore i kitea
Kua mate noa atu
I te awa i Pikopiko-i-whiti
Ma te maranga mai ai
Ko hiku-nuku e!
Tā tāua rangi!*
King of the forest birds, chief of the parakeets that guard *Tāne's* mighty woods, *Tāne's* sacred resting place (listen to my prayer!) *Tāne* (the tree) stood erect, amidst the forest shades, but now he's fallen. The trunk of *Tāne* has been severed from the butt; the stump of the tree felled to build this house stands yonder in the sacred resting place. The branchy tree-top, the leafy head has been cut off; it lies yonder in the Vast-Forest-of-*Tāne*. I have performed my ceremonies of propitiation; I have appealed to the spirits of our priestly ancestors and to the sacred ones. I have struck these timbers with mallet and chisel; I have struck them with the axe of the Sounding-Seas. I have mounted upon the great foaming girdle of the sea-god *Tangaroa*, the waves beaten down and divided by the canoe *Nuku-tai-maroro*, I am seeking, searching for the descendants of the children of *Rata*, to carve these timbers for me. I found them not; they were slain at the river *Pikopiko-i-whiti*. Oh ancient ones; return and aid me on this our sacred day.

Like all things in Maoridom, the origins of carving are set in myth and tradition, although there are different tribal versions. According to the tribes of the east coast of the North Island, *Ruatepupuke* journeyed to the domain of *Tanga-roa*, god of the sea, and there obtained the art of wood carving. The following *whakapapa* (genealogy) shows the relationship of the central figures in this story:

RANGINUI = PAPATUANUKU
|
Tangaroa
|
Poutu   Ikatere   Punga
|
Ruatepupuke
|
Manuruhi
|
Ruatepukenga

When *Manurihi's* son *Ruatepukenga* was growing up, he had a great fondness for seafood. *Manuruhi*, therefore, asked his father *Ruatepupuke* to give him a powerful fishhook. *Ruatepupuke* fashioned a special stone into a fishhook and called it *Te Whatukura o Tangaroa* (the prized stone of Tangaroa). He warned *Manuruhi* not to go out alone and use the hook but to wait for him so that together they could catch the first fish and make an offering to the gods. After waiting for what seemed an eternity, *Manuruhi*, who was curious about the power of the fishhook, went and cast it out. Its power was very apparent from the amount of fish that *Manuruhi* caught. However, *Tangaroa* was not pleased with what *Manuruhi* had done. Not only had he used the name of *Tangaroa* without his blessing, but he had breached custom and ritual by failing to offer a sacrifice for his first catch. *Tangaroa* took *utu* (revenge) for these *hara* (sins) and changed *Manuruhi* into a bird.

Ruatepupuke began searching for his missing son. After calling at village after village and searching the beaches he sat down and wept for him. Then in an act of desperation he swam out to the spot where his son had been fishing and dived down. To his surprise he saw a village very much the same as a Maori village, with a spectacular

Figure 49. *Kūwaha pātaka*, storehouse doorway, Ngāti Paoa tribe. This *kūwaha* was probably carved with stone tools. The *taratara-a-kai* pattern is seen on the body and *rauponga* on the face of the figure. (84)

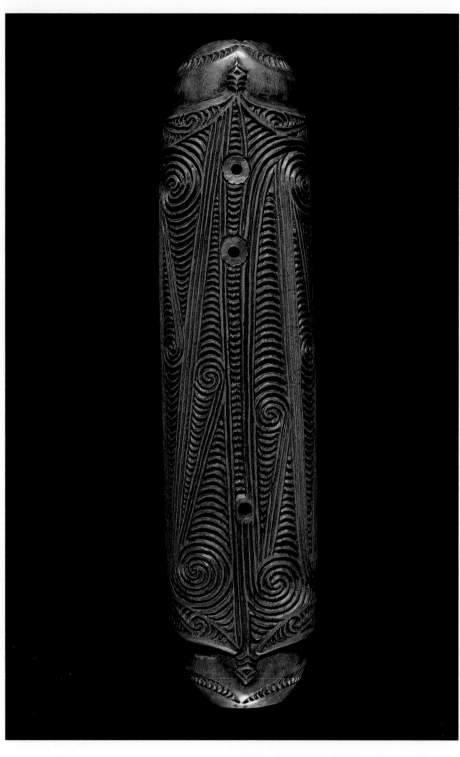

Figure 50. *Kōauau*, flute. Human figures were not always used to decorate small objects. The carving sometimes appears to be purely ornamental. (52)

house called *Huiteananui*. He peered into the house and saw the *poupou* (side posts) talking to each other. Then he saw that his son *Manuruhi* had been changed into the *tekoteko* (gable figure) of the house. His son's eyes glared pleadingly and earnestly at him.

Ruatepupuke now decided to take his own *utu* (revenge). From the talking *poupou* he learned that the people of the village were away and would not be returning until the evening, so he hid and waited. When they had returned and were asleep, *Ruatepupuke* commenced his revenge. After taking his son down he set fire to the house. When the people rushed out he struck them with his *patu* (club). All the *poupou* were burnt except four silent ones on the porch. *Ruatepupuke* grabbed these and the *tekoteko* of his son and hastened home. Thus it is to *Ruatepupuke* that we owe the origin of Maori carving because it was he who brought back into this world the silent *poupou* and the *tekoteko* image of his son, *Manuruhi*.

The many carved *whare whakairo* (carved meeting houses) are witnesses of this strong and continuous carving tradition. In former times, certain carvers were eagerly sought after to build meeting houses. Noted examples were the *tohunga whakairo* (master carvers) of the *Ngāti Tarāwhai* tribe of *Te Arawa*, who carved many meeting houses all over the country. The house *Tokopikowhakahau* is one example.

Today a carver feels a sense of achievement when he has completed a meeting house. To the Maori, apprenticeship is not a rigidly structured three-year course culminating in a certificate. In the words of master carver Lou Kereopa:

. . .the key to becoming a good carver is through a lot

of patience, perseverance and keeping an open mind. . .One can only learn from the past in order to mature and progress as a carver.

The apprenticeship of life, of experience, of time are the enduring factors.

Therefore, to look at a *poutoko-manawa* figure, a *pare*, a *wakahuia*, is to see and feel the experience of life that it communicates to us. Tai Pewhairangi, a *kaumātua* (respected elder) of the *Ngāti Porou* tribe, sums it up as follows:

They [*taonga*] carry within them the *mana* of the old people, and they are part of the line of descent which stretches from the most distant past and into the most distant future.

As one carver puts it:

The seasoned skill of the carver is manifested in the bold and confident cuts taken, mastering the shape and form which is complemented by the intricately flowing patterns of the *pakati*, (carving pattern) and *raperape* (carving pattern). With the rhythmic *paopao* cadence of the *patuki* (mallet) and *whao* (chisel), the richness of the carving unfolds. Then, looking upon the face of the *tekoteko*, uncovering the finely-etched lines of the *moko* (facial tattoo) which speak of its *whakapapa*, its *mana*, the carver, when it is completed, can say *Tihei Mauriora!*

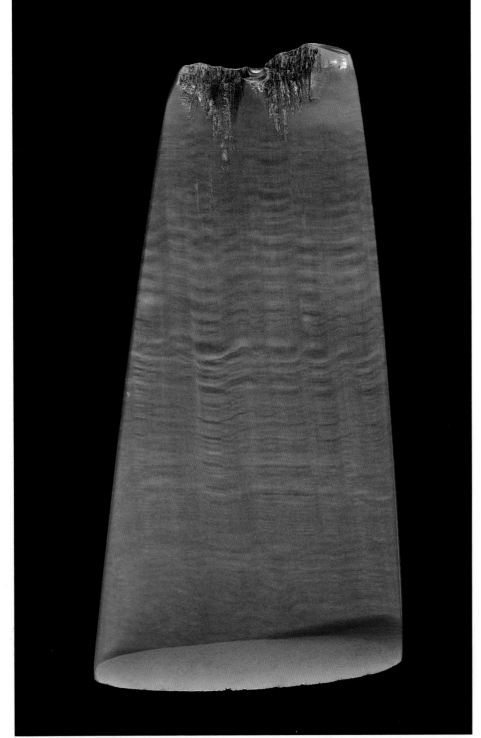

Figure 51. *Toki pounamu,* **greenstone adze,** Tai Tokerau district. *Pounamu* was prized by carvers above all other stone. (32)

W e a v i n g

As we view weaving produced during the nineteenth and early twentieth centuries, at a time when we are drawing closer to the year 2000, it may be timely to ask whether there is a thread of continuity in Maori weaving. Viewers may well ask how the weaving in this exhibition links the New Zealand Maori to both the past and future.

Weaving is interwoven with all aspects of Maori culture and is itself an essential part of the fabric of Maori culture and society.

The Polynesians who first settled *Aotearoa* arrived with knowledge of weaving and plaiting. Adaptation to climatic conditions and alternative materials forced the development of existing weaving techniques and the introduction of new ones, utilising the new materials such as *harakeke* (New Zealand flax; *Phormium tenax*), *pīngao* (*Demoschoenus spiralis*), *tī kōuka* (*Cordyline* sp.), and *kiekie* (*Freycinetia banksii*). These were readily available to meet the need to produce clothing better suited to the harsher conditions of New Zealand, and for containers for many purposes.

The colonial era in New Zealand saw further developments in Maori weaving. New materials and styles of clothing brought changes. The weaving in this exhibition is typical of that period. Cloaks featuring coloured wool oversewn on the traditional weaving, and small 'evening bags' with fringes reflect European influences.

What has remained unchanged by those influences is the intrinsic values. To many Maori weavers of this century, the values held by their ancestors towards weaving are just as important today as they were generations ago.

NGĀ MAHI

Far left: **Figure 52. Detail from sampler of traditional *raranga* patterns.** (124)

Left: **Figure 53. *Kaitaka, tāniko* cloak.** The weaver of this nineteenth century cloak was innovative and creative in her use of new and traditional materials. (141)

TE WHARE PORA

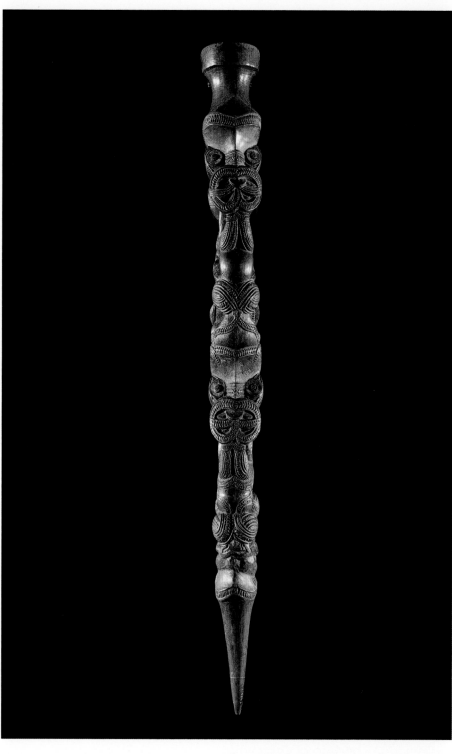

Above: **Figure 54. *Turuturu*, weaving peg.**
The weaving is suspended between two pegs. In the *whatu* technique, four weft threads are finger woven, interlocking the warps individually. (148)

Weaving is more than manual skills, more than producing a functional item, more than creating an item of beauty. Maori weaving is a vehicle that can link the past to the present and the present to the future. The threads of continuity are the Maori values. These threads can be in many shades. The strongest is the *wairua* (the spiritual aspect).

Customs, traditions, history, music, oratory, legends, and the needs of *iwi* (tribe), *hapū* (subtribe) and *whānau* (family) are all drawn together within an individual who becomes a weaver, who creates or weaves not for herself alone, but for the *mana* (prestige) of the people.

This exhibition could well conjure up an image of a Maori weaver as a dark-skinned woman seated at a loom. Nothing could be further from the truth. Not only is a loom never used (Maori weaving is done without spinning wheel, needle or loom), but it is now being produced by men and by New Zealanders of all races.

Maori weaving uses a number of techniques. This exhibition features the techniques of *whatu*, employed to weave the cloaks and small fibre bags; *tāniko*, a different weaving technique used on the borders of some of the cloaks and to give another decorative dimension to the small fibre bags; and *raranga*, the basket-making technique, which has best survived the influences of the changing times.

At the time the weaving in this exhibition was created, the pieces were not regarded as 'art works' for exhibiting. They were woven as functional objects, and were used to warm the body or carry objects. They are revered now not only because they are of another time, but because their *mauri* (life force) has been enriched with experience, and because the workmanship is of a quality that is not normally produced today.

Above: **Figure 55. *Poi*, poi ball.** *Poi* are twirled, twisted and struck to accompany songs and chants. This *poi* is unusual in its size, style and artistry. (56)

Left: **Figure 56. Detail of kahu-huruhuru, feather cloak.** Kākā and tūī feathers have been woven into the cloak. (139)

Workmanship and quality are perhaps more easily understood than *mauri*. *Mauri* is often defined as 'life force'. English words cannot convey the true feeling of *mauri*. It is a concept that requires thorough study if its full significance is to be understood and appreciated. Maori weavers regard all their natural weaving material as possessing a *mauri*. As with humans, the *mauri* is weaker at certain times and stronger at other times. The materials are gathered when the *mauri* is in its optimum state. Periods of wind, frost, rain, and long dry spells all affect the *mauri*, and so *harakeke*, *pīngao* and *kiekie* are not gathered at these times. The plants are gathered when the time is right for them, just as the time must be right for the gatherer. A woman menstruating is deemed to be physically out of balance and so the time is 'not right' for her to be associated with materials for her weaving.

Everything is done in the right order according to time and season to ensure that the plants are cared for and the weaving will proceed without problems. The weaving traditions also protect the *mauri*, through the observation of customs that have been handed down from mother to daughter.

Once the material is gathered, the weaver then has a responsibility to ensure that it is given another dimension. So the gathered weaving material is woven into a basket or a cloak, or some other useful item that also brings visual pleasure to the recipient.

The finished piece is often welcomed into this world as a new creation with all due ceremony. Many weavings are named. They live their lives until their 'wearing out' reflects the completion of their life force. They are then returned to mother Earth to feed the soil to ensure the life cycle of the plants for future weaving.

Above left: **Figure 57. *Kete whakairo*, kit.** This *kete* was taken to England before 1833. An unusual feature is the inclusion of a slightly offset block of a different pattern on one side only. (125)

Below left: **Figure 58. *Kete tāniko*, kit.** The *tāniko* technique, originally used mainly in garments, has been adapted to bags for special occasions. The fringe adds to the ornamental effect. (134)

Above: **Figure 59. Detail from sampler of *raranga* patterns.** The *niho taniwha* pattern seen here is used by weavers of many tribes. (124)

Right: **Figure 60.** *Ngā whānau a Māhu,* **by Emmitt Aranga.** Carving in bone and whale ivory is a flourishing art form today. (156)

Far right: **Figure 61. Pendant, by Hepi Maxwell.** The tradition of carving precious ornaments in *pounamu* continues. (154)

TE AO HUR

The Ever-changing World

T*e Ao Hurihuri*

te ao huri ai ki tōna tauranga:

te ao rapu;

ko te huripoki e huri nei

I runga i te taumata o te kaha.

Te Ao Hurihuri
is a world revolving:
a world that moves forward
to the place it came from;
a wheel that turns
on an axle of strength.

The future of the Maori in the twentieth century can be seen in the reassertion of cultural identity and Maori *mana motuhake* (Maori spirituality set apart). This assertion of Maori cultural identity and Maori self-determination has taken many forms and is being manifested more fully in the political process of New Zealand.

The Maori, like the indigenous people of many other colonised nations, suffered as a result of the colonisation process. Strategies like amalgamation, assimilation, integration and Europeanisation were thought to be the way to improve the lot of the Maori people from the post-contact period through to the twentieth century.

From the early days of the nineteenth century the settler population, the colonisers, thought that the Maori could be 'civilised' through the process of acculturation and thus take a respectable place in the world. Civilisation was seen by some as aiding in the Christianising of the Maori, and conversely Christianity was seen by some as aiding in the civilisation of the Maori. In the first half of the twentieth century, Euro-

HURI

Above: **Figure 62. Painted panel, Manutuke church**, Rongowhakaata tribe. Traditional *kōwhaiwhai* patterns have long been used to decorate Maori Christian churches. These examples data from 1849, although they have been repainted. (106)

Right: **Figure 63. Carved slab**, Ngāti Tarāwhai, tribe, Te Arawa. Tene Waitere carved this panel for the Colonial Museum in 1899. It shows male and female tattoos. The oblique face was a departure from traditional practice. (151)

peanisation and acculturation were the desired policies for the Maori people.

By the mid-twentieth century, integration superseded policies like amalgamation and assimilation. In reality, however, these terms were often used interchangeably and disguised the fact that the government wanted to unite the Maori and *Pakeha* into a 'one nation, one people' society. The European colonists were trying to impose and reproduce their mother country and their European culture as *the* culture for the Maori people.

Out of this period of cultural assimilation there emerged a man with foresight and perception. He was Apirana Ngata, a leading Maori authority and politician of the *Ngāti Porou* tribe of the eastern coast of the North Island. Apirana Ngata wanted the Maori people to have the opportunities to participate fully in the economic, political, and social advantages that New Zealand had to offer, while at the same time retaining the traditions and heritage of their culture as a chiefly plume for their headdress. This, he believed, was the right direction for the Maori people in this ever-changing world of ours (*Te Ao Hurihuri*).

Today Apirana's words echo long and hard for the future aspirations of the Maori people. The Treaty of Waitangi, which was signed by many of the tribes of New Zealand and the representative of the Crown on 6 February 1840, lays the foundation for these hopes and aspirations. The Treaty of Waitangi was a sacred covenant, a social contract that was entered into by the Crown and the many tribes of New Zealand. This solemn contract comprised three sections. It guaranteed the Maori people equal rights as British citizens. It also guaranteed to them the *rangatiratanga* (chieftainship, control) over their lands and es-

Above: **Figure 64. *Kete muka,*
by Erenora Puketapu-Hetet.** Maori weavers use traditional techniques and materials to make objects for use in the modern world. (153)

Right: **Figure 65. *Hei Matau,*
by Moanaroa Zagrobelna.** Modern pendants are often based on traditional forms. Here, a stylised fishhook is carved in whale ivory rather than *pounamu.* (157)

tates, forests, fisheries and other properties that they may have possessed collectively or individually, provided it was their wish to retain them.

The Maori people entered into this Treaty with dignity and honour. Many chiefs of New Zealand signed the Treaty believing that the Crown would honour it in full. As can be seen in the tide of history, this Treaty was not honoured; rather it was seen as a thorn in the side of the Crown, and often given no validity in the judicial or legislative bodies of New Zealand. New Zealand's history is one of land alienation, land confiscation and broken promises by the Crown and its representatives.

When the Treaty of Waitangi has been invoked on numerous occasions since 1840, it has invariably been dismissed as a legal 'nullity' having no authority in the courts of the land. Today, however, the Treaty is taking on a new meaning. It is the 'Magna Carta' of Maori constitutional rights and the very cornerstone of biculturalism in New Zealand. Through the Treaty the Maori language, heritage and culture are given recognition, respect and dignity in the same way that other different and diverse cultures should be. With the recent decisions giving effect to the Treaty, New Zealand seems to be on track to put right the wrongs and injustices of the past. If the New Zealand government is committed to this task, then both Maori and *Pakeha* can look to the future with hope and confidence.

Therefore, this exhibition carries our pain, sweat, tears and joy as expressed through our *taonga* (treasures). The hope is that you may feel the *ihi* (prestige), *wehi* (fear) and *mana* (power) of these treasures and that perhaps you too can understand the messages and experiences of life that they communicate to us. Our artwork, our treasures, are a reflection of us as people; we believe that they possess a *mauri* (life force) and *wairua* (spirit) all of their own.

As Sidney Mead, a noted Maori elder and scholar and authority on Maori art, has aptly expressed it:

Art is for people, is about people, and is people;

Art should 'live' with the people because it is a mea-sure of our human existence and of our quest for dignity in life. . .the art is intimately linked to our sense of worth and of dignity and most of all we are attached to our artworks; we love them and respect them.

Two *whakataukī* (proverbs) come to mind that express the feelings of the Maori people about their artworks, their culture, their way of life:

E tipu, e rea, mōi ngā rā o tōu ao;
Ko tō ringa, ki ngā rākau a te Pākehā, hei ara mō tō tinana;
Ko tō ngākau, ki ngā taonga a ō tīpuna Māori, hei tikitiki mō tō mahuna;
Ko tō wairua ki tō Atua, nāna nei ngā mea katoa.
                    —Apirana Ngata
(Grow, Oh tender child in the days of your life.
Your hand to the tools of the *pakeha* [non-Maori people] to provide physical sustenance
Your heart to the treasures of your ancestors as a topknot for your head
Your spirit to your god to whom all things belong.)

He toi whakairo, he mana tangata.
(Where there is artistic excellence there is human dignity.)

Therefore it is with great pride and dignity that we ask you to join us on a journey that will bring both past and present together through the beauty and history of our *taonga*. As with the "*Te Maori*" exhibition that travelled to the United States, we invite you to experience with us the *mana* of our past and present so that together we can face the future.

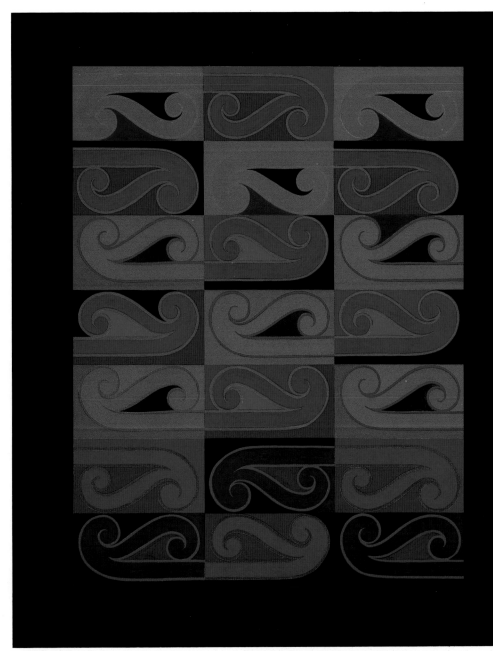

Figure 66. *Kahurangi*, by Sandy Adsett. Traditional *kōwhaiwhai* patterns provide inspiration for modern painters. (160) (Photograph, National Art Gallery.)

No reira,
E ngā taonga a Kui mā, a Koro mā.
Tēnei te mihi atu, te powhiri atu, te tangi atu ki a koutou.
Maranga mai, maranga mai!
Therefore, to the treasures of my forebears, I greet you, I welcome you, I cry for you and hope that you will rise and be with us in this ever-revolving world of ours.

NOTE ON CATALOGUE ENTRIES

For each *taonga*, information is given (where known) in the following order.

Name in Maori and English
Tribe
Locality
Period
Material, dimensions
Museum number, collection, date acquired

Sidney Mead's style periods have been adopted as an indication of the age of the objects. These are:

Ngā Kākano	A.D. 900–1200
Te Tipunga	A.D. 1200–1500
Te Puāwaitanga	A.D. 1500–1800
Te Huringa I	A.D. 1800–1900
Te Huringa II	A.D. 1900 to present

Te Huringa I was a time of great change in Maori culture and society. The *taonga* attributed to *Te Huringa I* reflect these changes and some can be fairly precisely dated.
Accordingly, *Te Huringa I* has been divided into three: early, middle, and late. The boundaries are not sharply defined, but very broadly the divisions cover the periods 1800–1840, 1840–1870, and 1870—1900.

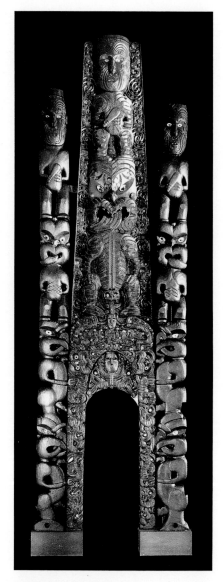

1. *Waharoa* (gateway)
Ngāti Tarāwhai tribe of Te Arawa
Te Huringa II
Wood, 640 cm high (central piece)
ME 1771a–c
This gateway was carved by Neke Kapua and his sons Tene and Eramiha for the Christchurch Exhibition of 1906. It was commissioned by the Government and carved in Wellington from a huge slap of *tōtara* brought from the central North Island. The carvers erected the gateway in Christchurch where it formed the entrance to a model Maori village.

2. *Poutokomanawa* (centre post figure)
Ngāti Kahungunu tribe
Wairoa, northern Hawkes Bay
Te Huringa I (middle or late)
wood, 137.5 cm high
ME 13339, acquired 1950
See figure 12 (left)

3. *Poutokomanawa* (centre post figure)
style of Ngāti Kahungunu tribe
Te Huringa I (middle or late)
wood, 86.6 cm high
ME 10955
See figures 12 (centre) & 13

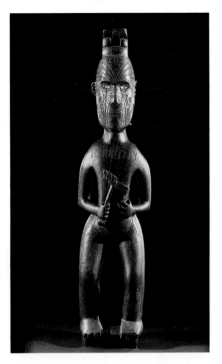

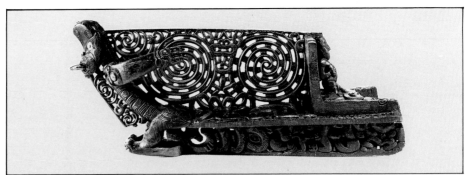

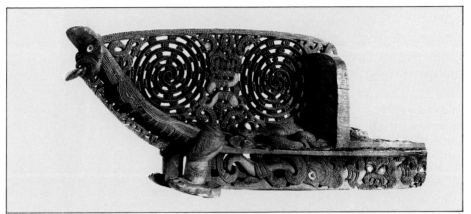

4. *Poutokomanawa* (centre post figure)

Ngāti Kahungunu tribe
Te Huringa I (middle or late)
wood, 149 cm high
ME 10958, Hill collection, acquired 1905
See figure 12 (right)

The name of the figure, IHUTAPU, is carved across the chest. Ihutapu was an ancestor of the Ngāti Kahungunu tribe.

5. *Waka* (model canoe)

Te Huringa I
wood, 207 cm long
OLD s10
Oldman collection, repatriated 1948
See figure 8.

This model is in the style of a *waka taua* (war canoe), but the *tauihu* (prow) is more like that of a *waka tētē* (fishing canoe).

6. *Tauihu* (war canoe prow) (top)

Te Huringa I (middle)
wood, 158 cm long, 64 cm high
OLD s248, Oldman collection, repatriated 1948

7. *Tauihu* (war canoe prow) (bottom)

Ngāti Porou tribe
Te Huringa I (early)
wood, 118.5 cm long, 50 cm high
WEB 1202, Webster collection, repatriated 1958
See figure 9.

This prow is carved in the style of the Ngāti Porou tribe. It is said to have been collected on Kapiti Island, where it would have been in the possession of the Ngāti Toa tribe. They had a number of canoes of Ngāti Porou origin.

8. *Taurapa* (war canoe sternpost)

style of Arawa tribes
Te Huringa I (middle)
wood, 147 cm long
ME 13455, acquired 1977

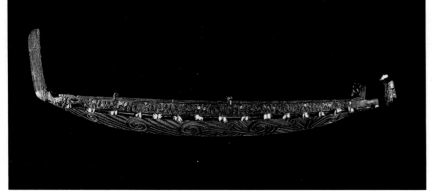

9. *Taurapa* (canoe sternpost)
Ngāti Pikiao tribe of Te Arawa
Okere, Lake Rotoiti, Rotorua
Te Puāwaitanga
wood, 65.1 cm long
ME 1829, acquired 1918
This delicately carved sternpost is probably from a small lake canoe.

10. *Taurapa* (war canoe sternpost)
Ngāti Toa tribe
Te Huringa I (early)
wood, 205 cm high
ME 14331, acquired 1981
See figures 15 & 46a, 46b.

This sternpost is said to be from the canoe Kahutia-te-rangi, one of the fleet used by the warrior chief Te Rauparaha in his campaigns against South Island tribes in the 1820s and 1830s. It was purchased from the Ngāti Toa tribe in 1861 by James McKay (then Assistant Native Secretary).

11. *Hoe* (paddle) (left)
Te Huringa I (early or middle)
wood, 165 cm long
WEB 289, Webster collection, repatriated 1958

12. *Hoe* (paddle) (right)
style of Te Ati Awa tribe
Te Huringa I (early)
wood, 170 cm long
WEB 1747, Webster collection, repatriated 1958
See figure 17.

13. *Tatā* or *tīheru* (bailer)
probably Rongowhakaata tribe
Poverty Bay area
Te Huringa I (middle)
wood, 46 cm long
ME 590, Hamilton collection, acquired 1904
According to Hamilton, this bailer was named Pororangi, after a chieftainess. It was one of a pair, both named.

14. *Tatā* or *tīheru* (bailer)
Te Huringa I (middle)
wood, 44 cm long
OLD 48, Oldman collection, repatriated 1948
(formerly Lord Ranfurly collection)

15. *Matau* (fishhook)
style of Kai Tahu tribe
Te Huringa I (early)
wood, bone, fibre, 12.7 cm long
OLD 105, Oldman collection, repatriated 1948
See figure 16.

16. *Mahe* (fishing sinker)
Te Puāwaitanga
greywacke
7.3 cm long, 4.7 cm diameter
OLD 564b
Oldman collection, repatriated 1948
Carved sinkers are rare, and were probably used in fishing ritual.

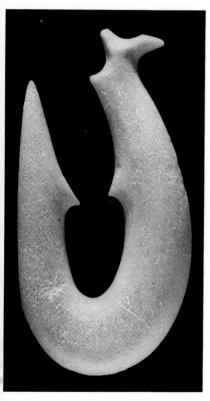

17. *Matau* (fishhook)
Te Puāwaitanga
bone, 7.7 cm long
ME 7939, Bollons collection, acquired 1931
See figure 6.

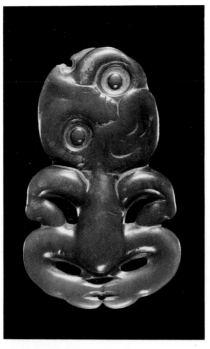

18. *Hei tiki* (neck pendant)
Te Huringa I (early)
nephrite, 8.1 cm long
ME 12925, acquired 1974

This *hei tiki* was once in the collection of Sir David Munro, first Speaker of the New Zealand House of Representatives. He would have acquired it in the mid-nineteenth century.

19. *Hei tiki* (neck pendant)
Te Puāwaitanga
nephrite, 12.3 cm long
ME 12842, repatriated 1972

20. *hei tiki* (neck pendant)
Te Huringa I (early)
nephrite, 13.8 cm long
OLD 1031, Oldman collection, repatriated 1948
See figure 3.

This *hei tiki* is said to have been taken to England in 1847 by Mr Elliot Macnaghten, Chairman of the East India Company, who had acquired it in India.

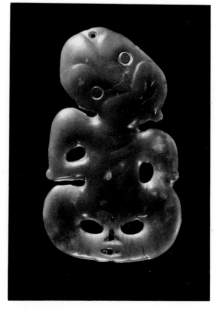

21. *Hei tiki* (neck pendant)
Te Puāwaitanga
nephrite, 12.1 cm long
ME 13171, acquired 1975
This *hei tiki* is said to have been collected by a Norwegian whaler.

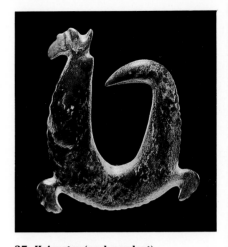

27. *Hei matau* (neck pendant)
Tai Tokerau tribes
Whangaroa
Te Puāwaitanga
nephrite, 4.7 cm long, 4.2 cm wide
WEB 400, Webster collection, repatriated 1958

22. Pendant (above)
Kai Tahu tribe
Ruapuke Island, Foveaux Strait
Te Puāwaitanga
bowenite, 14.2 cm long
ME 4937, Bollons collection, acquired 1931
Pendants such as this one and cat. no. 23, in the form of stylised birds, are found mainly in the southern South Island. In both these examples the stone has been exposed to heat.

23. Pendant (centre)
Kai Tahu tribe
Hakataramea, Otago
Te Puāwaitanga
bowenite, 16.6 cm long
ME 610, Hamilton collection, acquired 1904
See figure 11.

24. *Kapeu* (ear pendant)
Te Puāwaitanga
nephrite, 12.3 cm long
OLD 95a, Oldman collection, repatriated 1948

25. *Kapeu* (ear pendant)
Tai Tokerau tribes
Kaikohe, Northland
Te Puāwaitanga
nephrite, 7.2 cm long
ME 12492, acquired 1971

This pendant once belonged to Hone Toia, a northern chief whose tribal affiliations were with Te Mahurehure, Ngāti Te Rauawe and Ngāti Korokoro.

26. *Kuru* (ear pendant)
Te Puāwaitanga
nephrite, 5.5 cm long
ME 14967
This pendant provides a good illustration of a perforation made with a stone-tipped drill.

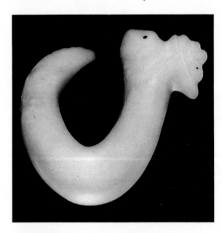

28. *Hei matau* (neck pendant)
Kai Tahu tribe
Kaiapoi area
Te Puāwaitanga
nephrite, 6.5 cm long, 5.2 cm wide
ME 608, Hamilton collection, acquired 1904

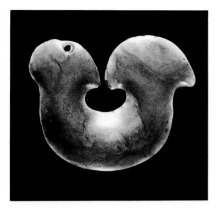

29. *Hei matau* (neck pendant)
Te Huringa I (early)
nephrite, 8.3 cm long, 10.3 cm wide
OLD 96, Oldman collection, repatriated 1948
See figure 22.

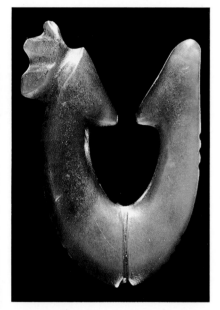

30. *Matau pounamu* (nephrite fishhook)
Te Puāwaitanga
nephrite, 3.1 cm long, 2.1 cm wide
OLD 97, Oldman collection, repatriated 1948
A fishhook such as this may have been either
for fishing ritual or a personal ornament.

31. *Pōria* (bird tethering ring)
Te Huringa I (early)
nephrite, 4.1 cm long, 3.5 cm wide
ME 14175, Newman collection, acquired 1971
Plain bone rings were used to tether tame
decoy birds, particularly *kākā* (New Zealand
parrots), by the leg. More elaborate forms, and
nephrite examples such as this one, were worn
as neck or ear pendants.

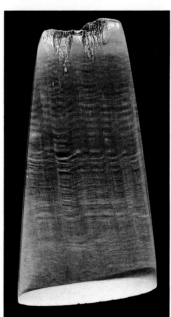

32. *Toki pounamu* (nephrite adze blade)
Tai Tokerau tribes
Bay of Islands
Te Puāwaitanga
nephrite, 17.5 cm long
ME 12860, acquired 1972
See figure 51.

Large nephrite adzes were important wood
carving tools. Perforated examples such as
this and cat. no. 33 were often hafted in
elaborately carved handles and became *toki
poutangata* like cat. no. 75.

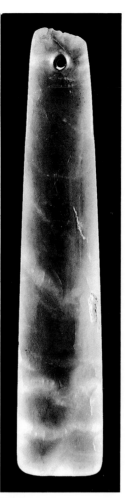

33. *Toki pounamu* (nephrite adze blade)
Te Huringa I (early)
nephrite, 31.3 cm long
ME 2965, Turnbull collection, acquired 1913
See figure 42.

34. *Toki pounamu* (nephrite adze blade)
Te Tipunga
nephrite, 23.5 cm long
OLD 119, Oldman collection, repatriated 1948
See figure 7.

The shaping of this adze blade to facilitate
hafting is a typically East Polynesian feature
and suggests that the blade was made during
Te Tipunga style period.

35. *Toki* (adze blade)
Ngāti Kahungunu tribe
Hawkes Bay
Te Puāwaitanga
argillite, 26 cm long
ME 3816, Purvis Russell collection, acquired 1921

Massive adze blades of this type, sometimes
with ornamental spirals as in this example, had
a limited distribution centring on Hawkes Bay.

36. *Toki* (adze blade)
Tainui tribal area
Te Kuiti
Te Tipunga
metamorphosed mudstone, 30 cm long
ME 4058

The sharply rectangular section, lashing grip
and "horns" are typically East Polynesian.
However, some blades like this one were
passed down as heirlooms and used on
ceremonial occasions.

37. *Toki* (adze blade)
Muaūpoko tribal area
Horowhenua, southern North Island
Ngā Kākano or Te Tipunga
metasomatised argillite, 56.6 cm long
ME 6300, Buller collection, acquired 1913

The rectangular section and lashing grip are
typically East Polynesian. Exceptional stone
working skill was necessary to make an adze
blade of this size.

38. *Toki* (adze blade)
Muaūpoko tribal area
Horowhenua, southern North Island
Ngā Kākano or Te Tipunga
metasomatised mudstone, 25 cm long
ME 13267, acquired 1975

This type of adze blade, known as a "hogback", is also characteristically East Polynesian. Such adzes were probably used in canoe building.

39. *Toki* (adze blade)
Kai Tahu tribal area
Southland
Te Tipunga
hard sandstone, 41.5 cm long
ME 812, Aston collection, acquired about 1904

This variant of a widespread East Polynesian style is found only in southern New Zealand. It may be attributed to the Waitaha tribe, who preceded Kai Tahu in the region.

40. Amulet
Kai Tahu tribal area
Orepuke, Southland
Te Tipunga
argillite, 9.2 cm long
ME 654, Hamilton collection, acquired 1904

This unique amulet has both East Polynesian and Maori features. It was probably a pendant. It may be attributed to the Waitaha tribe, who preceded Kai Tahu in the region.

41. Breast pendant
Port Underwood, Marlborough
Ngā Kākano
serpentine, 13.2 cm diameter
ME 14424, Guard collection, acquired 1984

This form of breast pendant may be derived from the pearl shell breast plates of tropical Polynesia, which it closely resembles in shape. This example is attributed to the Waitaha tribe, earlier inhabitants of this region.

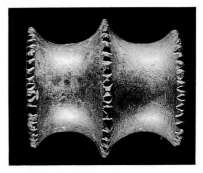

42. Necklace unit
Ngāti Kahungunu tribal area
Hawkes Bay
Te Tipunga
serpentine, 4.7 cm long, 3.9 cm diameter
ME 633, Hamilton collection, acquired 1904
See figure 5.

This style of ornament was brought to New Zealand by the settlers from East Polynesia. Originally part of a necklace, large stone units of this type were sometimes handed down as heirlooms and worn as single pendants. This example probably belonged to members of an earlier tribe which occupied the region before Ngāti Kahungunu.

43. *Pūtōrino* (bugle-flute)
Te Huringa I (early)
wood, fibre, 52 cm long
WEB 585, Webster collection, repatriated 1958

This flute is believed to have been collected before 1838.

44. *Pūtōrino* (bugle-flute) (left)
Te Huringa I (early)
wood, fibre, 57.5 cm long
OLD 1039, Oldman collection, repatriated 1948
See figure 44.

45. *Pūtōrino* (bugle-flute) (right)
Te Puāwaitanga
wood, fibre, 48 cm long
OLD 26, Oldman collection, repatriated 1948
This flute is believed to have been collected about 1845.

47. *Nguru* (flute)
Te Puāwaitanga
wood, 14.9 cm long
WEB 1887, Webster collection, repatriated 1958
The small inset human tooth is a very rare decorative feature.

49. *Nguru* (flute)
Te Huringa I (early)
sea mammal ivory, 9.9 cm long
WEB 1888, Webster collection, repatriated 1958

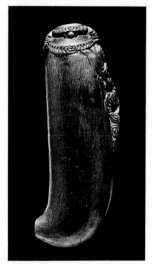

46. *Nguru* (flute)
Te Huringa I (early)
wood, 15.6 cm long
OLD 22, Oldman collection, repatriated 1948

48. *Nguru* (flute)
Ngāti Raukawa tribe
Te Puāwaitanga
wood, 11.5 cm long
ME 2288, Buller collection, acquired 1913
This flute was presented to Sir Walter Buller by Ihakara Tukumaru Te Hokowhitu-Kuri in the nineteenth century, after being handed down through several generations of the Patu-Kopuru hapū of Ngāti Raukawa.

50. *Nguru* (flute)
Te Puāwaitanga
serpentine, 11 cm long
OLD 172, Oldman collection, repatriated 1948
See figure 10.

51. *Kōauau* (flute)
Te Puāwaitanga
wood, 14.1 cm long
WEB 797, Webser collection, repatriated 1958

53. *Kōauau* (flute) (left)
Te Huringa I (early)
bone, 15.3 cm long
ME 10721
See figure 34.

54. *Kōauau* (flute) (right)
Te Huringa I (early)
bone, fibre, 15.2 cm long
OLD 566, Oldman collection, repatriated 1948

56. *Poi awe* (poi ball)
Te Huringa I
fibre, dog hair, 10.2 cm diameter
ME 150
See figure 55.

This poi consists of netting of New Zealand flax, stuffed with *tāhuna* (down of *raupo*). It is ornamented with dog hair tassels and god's eye decoration made from *kiekie* and red woollen yarn.

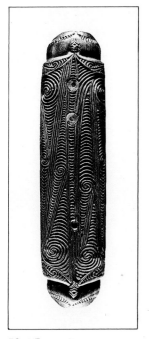

52. *Kōauau* (flute)
Te Huringa I (early)
wood, 17.7 cm long
ME 2514, acquired 1912
See figure 50.

55. *Kōauau* (flute)
style of Tai Tokerau tribes
Te Huringa I (early)
wood, 20.3 cm long
OLD 35, Oldman collection, repatriated 1948

57. *Taiaha or hani* (ceremonial and fighting staff)
probably Whanganui tribes
Te Huringa I (middle)
wood, 170.9 cm long
ME 1246, Handley collection, acquired 1905
The name of this taiaha is Te Ringa Mahi Kai.

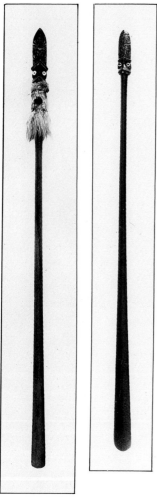

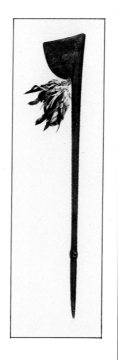

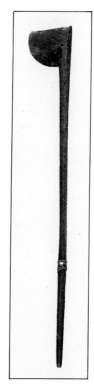

58. *Taiaha* or *hani* (ceremonial and fighting staff) (left)

Ngāti Paoa tribe
Te Huringa I (early)
wood, kaka feathers, dog hair, 167.3 cm long
ME 1864, Mair collection, acquired 1909

This *taiaha* belonged to Tekopara, a chief of Ngāti Paoa. During a visit to Rotorua in 1827, he murdered a man of Ngāti Pikiao. He and his party were immediately attacked in retaliation at Tumoana and the *taiaha* was taken by Te Tokoaitua of Ngāti Whakaue. In 1840 it was returned to Ngāti Paoa by Hakaraia Mahuika as a peace offering from the Arawa people.

59. *Taiaha* or *hani* (ceremonial and fighting staff) (right)

Ngāti Kahungunu tribe
Omahu, Hawkes Bay
Te Huringa I (middle)
wood, 140.6 cm long
ME 2424, Buller collection, acquired 1913
See figure 26.

This *taiaha* belonged to Renata Kawepo, a famous chief of Ngāti Te Upokoiri hapū of Ngāti Kahungunu.

60. *Tewhatewha* (long fighting club) (left)

Ngāti Awa tribe of Mataatua
Te Huringa I (early)
wood, hawk feathers, 128.9 cm long
ME 1861, Mair collection, acquired 1909

This *tewhatewha* is named Te Mautaranui, after the famous Ngāti Awa chief of that name. In 1832 Te Mautaranui was killed by his father-in-law, Tuakiaki of Ngāti Kohatu, with this *tewhatewha*. Many tribes joined Ngāti Awa in avenging his death. Te Mautaranui was given to Captain Gilbert Mair in 1866 by the famous Ngāti Awa carver Wepiha Apanui, grandson of Te Mautaranui.

61. *Tewhatewha* (long fighting club) (right)

probably Tainui tribes
Te Huringa I (middle)
wood, hawk feathers, 150.4 cm long
ME 383, Hammond collection, acquired 1904

62. *Tewhatewha* (long fighting club)

probably Tai Hauāuru tribes
Te Huringa I (middle)
wood, 122.5 cm long
ME 14, Butterworth collection, acquired 1904

63. *Hoeroa* (ceremonial staff)

Te Huringa I (early)
whalebone, 132.1 cm long
OLD 164, Oldman collection, repatriated 1948
See figure 19.

67. *Mere* (nephrite club)
Te Puāwaitanga
nephrite, fibre, 35.7 cm long
WEB 1096, Webster collection, repatriated 1958

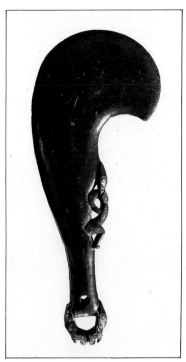

64. *Pouwhenua* (long weapon) (left)
Te Huringa I (early)
wood, 178.2 cm long
WEB 906, Webster collection, repatriated 1958
(formerly Buller collection)
See figure 35.

65. *Pouwhenua* (long weapon) (right)
Te Huringa I (early)
wood, 171.3 cm long
OLD 167, Oldman collection, repatriated 1948

66. *Mere* (nephrite club)
Ngāi Tama and Ngāti Awa of Mataatua
Te Puāwaitanga
nephrite, 31.3 cm long
ME 2112, Buller collection, acquired 1913
This *mere* belonged to Eru Tamaikoha Te
Ariari and was used during the wars of the
1860s.

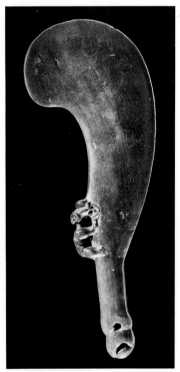

68. *Wahaika* (short club)
Te Puāwaitanga or Te Huringa I (early)
wood, 41.2 cm long
WEB 510, Webster collection, repatriated 1958
See figure 38.

69. *Wahaika* (short club)
Te Huringa I (early)
wood, 41 cm long
OLD 1054, Oldman collection, repatriated 1948.

70. *Wahaika* (short club)
Te Huringa I (early)
whalebone, 41 cm long
OLD 62, Oldman collection, repatriated 1948

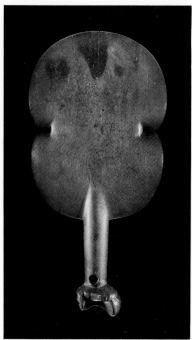

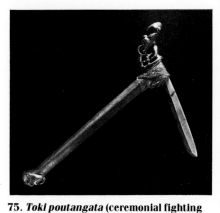

75. *Toki poutangata* (ceremonial fighting adze)
Te Puāwaitanga
wood, nephrite, fibre, 48.5 cm long
OLD 491, Oldman collection, repatriated 1948
See figure 21.

71. *Kotiate* (short club)
Te Puāwaitanga
wood, 33 cm long
OLD 80, Oldman collection, repatriated 1948
This is one of several Maori *taonga* said to have been taken to England by Captain James Wilson of the *Duff* in 1798. The *Duff* did not visit New Zealand, and Wilson probably obtained his Maori items in Sydney.

73. *Patu parāoa* (whalebone club)
Ngāti Maniapoto of Tainui
Te Huringa I (early)
whalebone, 39.6 cm long
ME 5007
This club is said to have belonged to Epiha (also known as Tokohihi), a fighting chief of the Waikato, and to have been taken from a Maori killed in battle in about 1861.

76. *Pūtātara* (shell trumpet)
Tūhoe tribe of Mataatua
Urewera, central North Island
Te Puāwaitanga/Te Huringa I
shell, wood, fibre, 24.5 cm long
WEB 1059, Webster collection, repatriated 1958
This trumpet, named Te Umu Kohukohu, was given to a European visitor in 1906 by Te Whenua-nui II. At that time it was about six generations old and was said to have been last used in 1867. The wooden mouthpiece may have been replaced at about that time.

72. *Patu onewa* (stone club)
Te Huringa I (early)
greywacke, 36.3 cm long
ME 14091, repatriated, acquired 1979
The wrist thong is modern.

74. *Kōtaha* (spear thrower)
Te Huringa I (early)
wood, 96.6 cm long
WEB 559, Webster collection, repatriated 1958

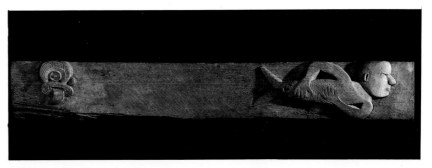

78. Part of the porch of a *wharenui* (meeting house).

Te Aitanga-a-Hauiti tribe of Ngāti Porou
Te Huringa I (late)

This house stood at Tolaga Bay on the east coast of the North Island in the late nineteenth century. Some of the timbers were acquired by the Museum as part of the Hill collection in 1905. Both *poupou* (side posts) and *heke* (rafters) are painted with the *kōwhaiwhai* patterns usually found on rafters. The portion of the *paepae* (threshold) is from the inner edge of the porch under the window. The figure on the *paepae* is a *marakihau* or merman.

Paepae (threshold)

Tolaga Bay house
wood, 232 cm wide
ME 8494

Heke rafter
Tolaga Bay house
wood, 429 cm long
ME 13218

Heke (rafter)
Tolaga Bay house
wood, 441 cm long
ME 13219

77. *Pou* (stockade post)

Rangitāne tribe
Rangiotu, Manawatu
Te Huringa I
wood, 270 cm high
ME 11160, acquired 1933

This stockade post is one of a group from Puketōtara Pā, Rangiotu, said to have been carved about 1830. It was presented to the Museum by Wiremu Te Aweawe.

Poupou (side post)
Tolaga Bay house
wood, 171 cm high
ME 4229a

Poupou (side post)
Tolaga Bay house
wood, 171 cm high
ME 4229b

79. Kumete (bowl)
Te Huringa I (middle)
wood, 90.5 cm long, 35.7 cm high
ME 4056
See figure 41.

80. Kumete (bowl)
Ngāti Kahungunu tribe
Waikare Village, near Wairoa, Hawkes Bay
Te Huringa I (middle)
wood. 80.5 cm long, 28.2 cm high
WEB 893, Webster collection, repatriated 1958

81. Tahā huahua (calabash)
Tai Rāwhiti or Ngāti Kahungunu tribes
East Coast or Hawkes Bay
Te Huringa I (late)
gourd, fibre, 40 cm high, 36 cm diameter
ME 1908, Hill collection, acquired 1905
See figure 37

Large calabashes such as this were used to store birds preserved in their own fat. They were often elaborately decorated and given as gifts. This example has a *papaki* covering.

82. Ipu (gourd for water)
Te Huringa I (early)
gourd, fibre, 16 cm diameter, 13 cm high
WEB 901, Webster collection, repatriated 1958

In former times, incised gourds such as this were not common. Gourd carving is now a popular art form.

Epa (front panel)
Te Awhi
wood, 172 cm high
ME 2006b

Epa (front panel)
Te Awhi
wood, 169 cm high
ME 2006c

83. Front of Te Awhi *pātaka* **(storehouse)**
Ngāti Pikiao of Te Arawa
Te Huringa I (early or middle)
See figure 25.

Te Awhi was carved from parts of a large canoe abandoned by the Ngā Puhi tribe during an intertribal campaign in 1823. It was carved about 1840 by Te Matara and others of Ngāti Pikiao, and erected at Maketu in the Bay of Plenty. It is said to have been named after the central part of Pukehina pā near Otamarakau. The four piles were carved to represent ancestors. The pile shown here is inscribed KO PUKEHINA. The carvings were acquired by the Museum in 1911; funds were made available to enable Tene Waitere to carve a replacement *pātaka* for the people of Maketu. Te Awhi appears in a water colour drawing by Robley in 1865 and in several photographs.

Kūwaha (doorway)
Te Awhi
wood, 192 cm high
ME 2006a

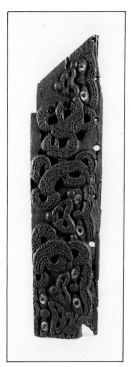

Epa (front panel)
Te Awhi
wood, 101 cm high
ME 2006d

Epa (front panel)
Te Awhi
wood, 132 cm high
ME 2006e

Epa (front panel)
Te Awhi
wood, 108 cm high
ME 2006f

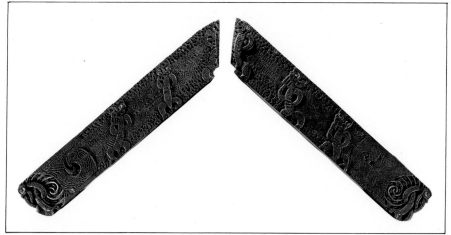

Maihi (bargeboard)
Te Awhi
wood, 299 cm long
ME 2006h

Maihi (bargeboard)
Te Awhi
wood, 296 cm long
ME 2006i

Amo (bargeboard support)
Te Awhi
wood, 75.5 cm high
ME 2006o

Amo (bargeboard support)
Te Awhi
wood, 74 cm high
ME 2006n

Epa (front panel)
Te Awhi
wood, 140 cm high
ME 2006g

Part of *pou aronui* (front supporting pile)
Te Awhi
wood, 99 cm high
ME 2006j

***Tekoteko* (gable figure)**
not originally part of Te Awhi
Te Arawa tribes
Te Huringa I (middle)
wood, 112.5 cm high
ME 10843

84. *Kūwaha* (doorway) and 2 *epa* (front panels) from a *pātaka* (storehouse)
Ngāti Paoa tribe
Miranda, Hauraki Gulf
Te Puāwaitanga
Webster collection, repatriated 1958
See figure 49.

These carvings were found buried in a swamp, where they had probably been hidden during inter-tribal warfare. They are thought to be about 250 years old. At one time they were in the possession of Sarah Bernhardt.

Part of *Kūwaha* (doorway)
wood, 86 cm high
WEB 484

***Epa* (front panel)**
wood, 73.4 cm high
WEB 482

***Epa* (front panel)**
wood, 99.5 cm high
WEB 483

85. *Kūwaha pātaka* (storehouse doorway)
Ngāti Awa tribe of Mataatua
Thornton, Bay of Plenty
Te Huringa I (early)
wood, 159.5 cm high
ME 12156, acquired 1932
See figure 36.
This carving was found in a swamp.

86. Part of *Kūwaha pātaka* (storehouse doorway)
style of Ngāti Kahungunu tribe
Te Huringa I (early)
wood, 92 cm high
OLD 489, Oldman collection, repatriated 1948

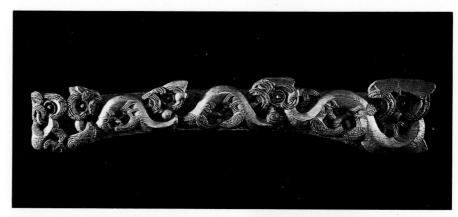

88. *Paepae* of a *pātaka* (threshold of a storehouse)
Te Ati Awa tribe
Waitara, north Taranaki
Te Puāwaitanga
wood, 150 cm long, 27.5 cm high
ME 4657, acquired 1930
See figure 47.

This carving was found in a swamp near Waitara. It is probably a *paepae* but some authorities have suggested that it may be a *pare* (lintel) or *maihi* (bargehoard).

87. *Paepae* or *rauawa* of a *pātaka* (threshold or sideboard of a storehouse)
Ngāti Pikiao tribe of Te Arawa
northern shore of Lake Rotoiti, Rotorua district
Te Huringa I (middle)
wood, 125.2 cm long, 42.8 cm high
ME 14355, acquired 1982

This is one of several carvings from a building said to have been carved by Tuterangiwhakaea. The nature of the building and the exact function of the carvings are no longer remembered. It seems likely that the building was a *pātaka* and that this carving was the *paepae* or one of the *rauawa*.

89. *Tekoteko* (gable figure)
style of Tai Rāwhiti tribes
Te Puāwaitanga
wood, 85.1 cm high
OLD 150, Oldman collection, repatriated 1948
See figure 45.

This is one of several Maori *taonga* said to have been taken to England by Captain James Wilson of the *Duff* in 1798. The *Duff* did not visit New Zealand, and Wilson probably obtained his Maori items in Sydney.

90. Fragment of a *pare* (lintel)
style of Bay of Plenty — East Coast tribes
Te Puāwaitanga
wood, 27.6 cm high, 44.2 cm wide
WEB 377, Webster collection, repatriated 1958
See figure 68 (back cover).

91. *Koruru* (gable mask)
Ngāti Porou tribe
vicinity of Tolaga Bay
Te Huringa I (late)
wood, 66.5 cm high
ME 286, Hill collection, acquired 1905

92. *Koruru* (gable mask)
style of Tūhoe tribe of Mataatua
Te Huringa I (middle)
wood, 55 cm high
OLD 143, Oldman collection, repatriated 1948
See cover and figure 43.

93. *Tekoteko* (gable figure)
Ngāti Tama tribe
Moawhango, central North Island
Te Huringa I (late)
wood, 85 cm high
ME 858, Hamilton collection, acquired 1904
The name of this Ngāti Tama ancestor, Rango, is incised on the chest.

94. *Tekoteko* (gable figure)
Ngāti Manawa tribe of Mataatua
Murupara district, central North Island
Te Huringa I (late)
wood, 96.4 cm high
ME 2411, Buller collection, acquired 1913
This figure represents a Ngāti Manawa ancestor, Te Aroakapa, and is said to be from a house named Ruatapu. The name of the ancestor is incised on the chest.

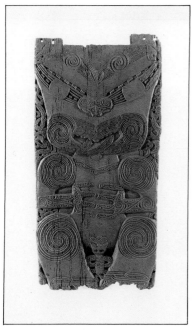

95. *Poupou* (side post from interior of house)

Tūhoe tribe of Mataatua
Ruatahuna, Urewera district
Te Huringa I (middle)
wood, 134 cm high
ME 1985, acquired 1910

This *poupou* may be from the fortified village of Mana-te-pa.

96. *Amo* (bargeboard support)

Tūhoe tribe of Mataatua
Urewera district
Te Huringa I (middle or late)
wood, 113 cm high
ME 1991, acquired 1910

97. *Whakawae* (doorjamb)

Ngāti Pikiao or Ngāti Tarāwhai tribe of Te Arawa
Taheke, Lake Rotoiti, Rotorua district
Te Huringa I (early)
wood, 94.6 cm high
WEB 1149, Webster collection, repatriated 1958
(formerly Hooper collection)

98. *Whakawae* (doorjamb)

Te Huringa I (early)
wood, 93.3 cm high
OLD 45, Oldman collection, repatriated 1948

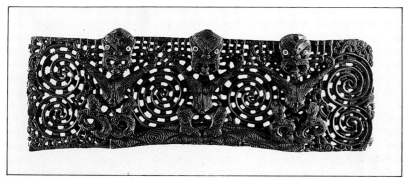

99. *Pare* or *Kōrupe* (lintel)
style of Ngāti Kahungunu tribe
Te Huringa I (middle)
wood, 108 cm wide, 36.4 cm high
OLD 579, Oldman collection, repatriated 1948
See figure 14.

100. *Pare* or *Kōrupe* (lintel)
style of Tai Tokerau tribes
Te Puāwaitanga
wood, 98 cm wide, 25 cm high
ME 13972, Hooper collection, repatriated 1977
This carving is sometimes interpreted as the
paepae of a small storehouse.

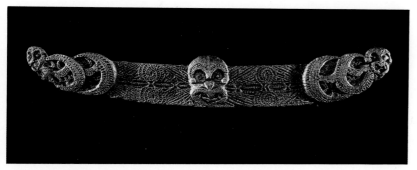

101. *Pare* or *kōrupe* (lintel)
Te Ati Awa tribe
Manukorihi swamp, Waitara, north Taranaki
Te Puāwaitanga
wood, 123.8 cm wide, 20.5 cm high
ME 5249, acquired about 1930

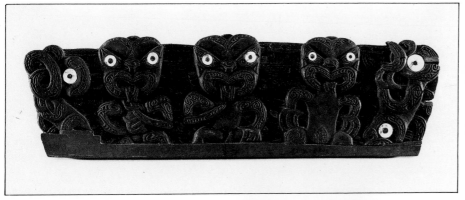

102. *Pare* **or** *kōrupe* **(lintel)**
Ngāti Kahungunu tribe
Omarunui, Hawkes Bay
Te Huringa I (middle)
wood, 91 cm wide, 26 cm high
ME 497, Hamilton collection, acquired 1904

103. Carvings from the front of a *wharenui*
(meeting house) named
Tokopikowhakahau

Te Huringa I (late)
See figure 24.

Tokopikowhakahau, named after an ancestor,
was carved by leading Ngāti Tarāwhai carver
Anaha Te Rahui and others for Karanama Te
Akatuku of Ngāti Raukawa. The house was
completed by 1886. It stood at Tapapa, on the
main road between Hamilton and Rotorua. Two
photographs show that the *koruru* included
here replaced an earlier *koruru* some time after
1892. The carvings came to the Museum in
1913 as part of the Turnbull collection.

Koruru **(gable mask)**
Tokopikowhakahau
wood, 120 cm high
ME 4200

Amo **(bargeboard support)**
Tokopikowhakahau
wood, 315 cm long
ME 2587b

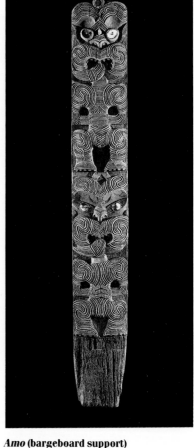

Amo **(bargeboard support)**
Tokopikowhakahau
wood, 313 cm long
ME 2587a

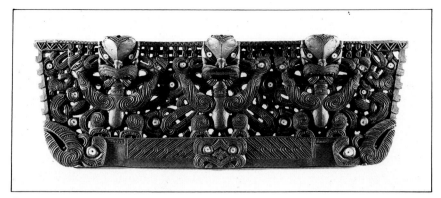

Pare (door lintel)
Tokopikowhakahau
wood, 148 cm wide, 49 cm high
ME 14970

Paepae (threshold)
Tokopikowhakahau
wood, 519 cm long
ME 8224

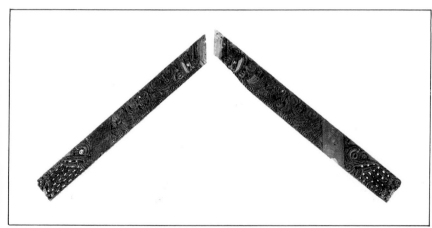

Maihi (bargeboard)
Tokopikowhakahau
wood, 515 cm long
ME 2585b

Maihi (bargeboard)
Tokopikowhakahau
wood, 514 cm long
ME 2585a

Whakawae (doorjamb)
Tokopikowhakahau
wood, 186 cm high
ME 2586b

Whakawae (doorjamb)
Tokopikowhakahau
wood, 187 cm high
ME 2586a

Fragment of *heke* **(rafter)**
Tokopikowhakahau
wood, 151 cm long
ME 2594a

Amo (?) (bargeboard support)
Poverty Bay house
wood, 184 cm high
ME 3775

Poupou (side post)
Poverty Bay house
wood, 186 cm high
ME 3777

104. Carvings from a *wharenui* (meeting house)

Poverty Bay
Te Huringa I (late)

These carvings from the Poverty Bay area on the east coast of the North Island are thought to have belonged to Wi Pere Halbert. The tribal affiliation is most likely to be with the Rongowhakaata, Te Aitanga-ā-Māhaki, or Ngai Tamanuhiri tribes. The carvings were acquired by the Museum in 1920.

Amo (?) (bargeboard support)
Poverty Bay house
wood, 184 cm high
ME 3774

Poupou (side post)
Poverty Bay house
wood, 184 cm high
ME 3776

Poupou (side post)
Poverty Bay house
wood, 184 cm high
ME 3778

Poupou (side post)
Poverty Bay house
wood, 184 cm high
ME 3779

Poutokomanawa (centre post figure)
Poverty Bay house
wood, 122 cm high
ME 3781

Poutokomanawa (centre post figure)
Poverty Bay house
wood, 122 cm high
ME 3783

105. Poutokomanawa (centre post figure)
style of Rongowhakaata tribe
Te Huringa I (early)
wood, 45.6 cm high
OLD 148, Oldman collection, repatriated 1948
See figure 20.

This free standing figure probably stood
against the base of the centre post of a house;
later *poutokomanawa* figures were carved in
the base of the post itself. This figure originally
had human hair attached to the head.

Painted panel
Manutuke church
wood, 298 cm high
ME 3143b

Painted panel
Manutuke church
wood, 298 cm high
ME 3143c

Painted panel
Manutuke church
wood, 298 cm high
ME 3143d

**106. Six panels from a church, painted
with *kōwhaiwhai* patterns**
Rongowhakaata tribe
Manutuke, Gisborne district
Te Huringa I (middle)
See figure 62.

These six panels from an old church at
Manutuke are thought to have been painted
about 1850. It is not known whether they were
poupou (side posts) or *heke* (rafters). They
were presented to the Museum by Rev. H.
Williams in 1913, and subsequently repainted
by T. Heberley.

Painted panel
Manutuke church
wood, 298 cm high
ME 3143a

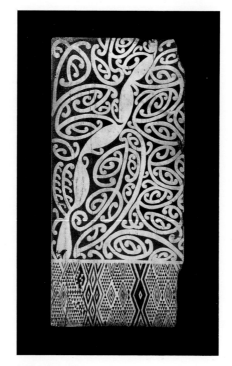

Painted panel
Manutuke church
wood, 149 cm high
ME 3143e

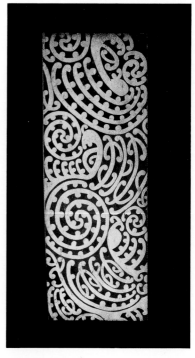

Painted panel
Manutuke church
wood, 149 cm high
ME 3143f

107. *Heru* (ornamental comb)

Te Puāwaitanga
wood, 8 cm long
WEB 529, Webster collection, repatriated 1958
See figure 29.

Combs were worn by men of high rank. Their heads were *tapu* and anything that came into contact with the head, such as a comb, also became *tapu* and had to be treated with great care.

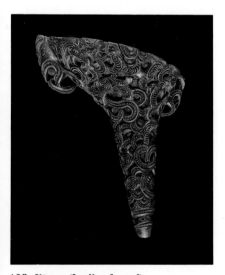

108. *Kōrere* (feeding funnel)

style of Tai Tokerau tribes
Te Huringa 1 (early)
wood, 16 cm deep
OLD 135, Oldman collection, repatriated 1948
See figure 28 & figure 30.

Elaborately carved funnels like this were used to feed a chief when his face was being tattooed. Food could not come into direct contact with his hands or face at such a time.

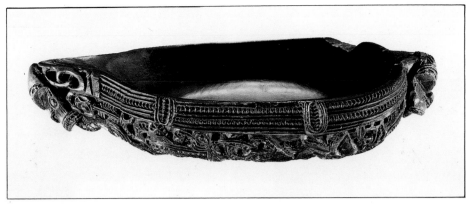

109. *Ipu* or *Kōrere* (pouring or feeding bowl)

Te Puāwaitanga
wood, 31.2 cm long
OLD 136, Oldman collection, repatriated 1948

The elaborate carving on this bowl suggests that it may be similar to a *kōrere* (chief's feeding funnel). This bowl is said to have been collected by Captain Cook, but no proof of this association has survived.

110. *Pou Whakairo* (carved post)

Te Ati Awa tribe
Huirangi swamp, Waitara, north Taranaki
Te Puāwaitanga
wood, 113 cm high
ME 14335, acquired 1981
See figure 4.

The use of this small, ornate carving is not known. It appears intended to stand upright and may have had a ritual function. It was uncovered by a mechanical ditch digger in 1967 and was in two pieces when it was found.

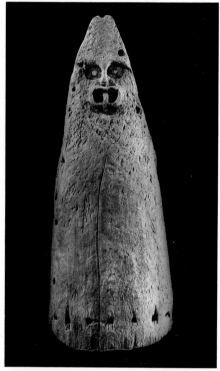

111. *Waka tūpāpaku* (part of burial chest)

Muaūpoko tribe
Lake Horowhenua, southern North Island
Te Puāwaitanga
wood, 77 cm high
BLACK 74, Black collection, acquired 1963
See figure 33.

This unusual carving was found with six similar but plain planks on the bed of Lake Horowhenua near Waikiekie Island Pā. It is thought to be part of a unique composite burial chest.

112. Waka tūpāpaku (burial chest)
Tai Tokerau tribes
Hokianga
Te Puāwaitanga
wood, 103 cm high
ME 1796, acquired about 1906
See figure 27.

This chest is thought to be from the Waimamaku area, Hokianga, with tribal affiliations to Ngāi Tu, Ngāti Teka, Te Roroa, Ngāti Pou. Carved chests of this type were used to hold the bones of important ancestors and were kept in caves. They are known only from a fairly small area of the northern North Island and are superb examples of the Tai Tokerau carving style.

113. Poupou (carved post)
Ngāti Tūwharetoa tribe
Poukawa, Tokaanu, Lake Taupo
Te Huringa I (middle)
wood, 261 cm high
ME 1867b

This is one of two posts carved by Iwikau (Te Heuheu Tukino III), who died in 1862. They were presented to the Museum by Te Heuheu Tukino V in 1909. It is not certain whether they are from a house or from a memorial structure or tomb.

114. Five poupou (carved posts)
Ngāti Tarāwhai tribe of Te Arawa
Ruato, Lake Rotoiti, Rotorua district
Te Huringa I (middle)
See figures 31 & 32.

These carvings formerly stood with three others at a tomb or memorial at Ruato. They may have been carved by Wero, a master carver of Ngāti Tarāwhai. When they were acquired for the Museum they had been lying under a shelter for some time and their original arrangement is not known.

Poupou
Ruato
wood, 230 cm high
ME 1439a

This carving depicts the ancestor, Te Rangitakaroro.

Poupou
Ruato
wood, 232 cm high
ME 1439c

Poupou
Ruato
wood, 231 cm high
ME 1439d

Poupou
Ruato
wood, 245 cm high
ME 1440a
This carving depicts the ancestor, Taporahitaua.

Poupou
Ruato
wood, 244 cm high
ME 1440b

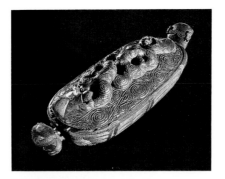

115. Wakahuia (treasure box)
style of Tai Rāwhiti tribes
Te Huringa I (middle)
wood, 76.7 cm long
OLD 3, Oldman collection, repatriated 1948
See figure 18.
Boxes of this kind were used to store precious ornaments and were suspended from the roof of a dwelling house. This one is exceptionally large.

116. Papahou (treasure box)
Te Puāwaitanga
wood, 35.6 cm long
OLD 11, Oldman collection, repatriated 1948
This is one of several Maori *taonga* said to have been taken to England by Captain James Wilson of the *Duff* in 1798. The *Duff* did not visit New Zealand, and Wilson probably obtained his Maori items in Sydney.

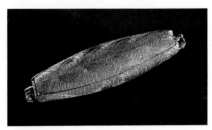

117. Wakahuia (treasure box)
Te Huringa I (early)
wood, 38.4 cm long
ME 3979
A crack in the side of this box has been neatly repaired by binding the pieces together with fine New Zealand flax cord. A small inlaid piece of nephrite is an unusual feature of the decoration.

118. Papahou (treasure box)
style of Tai Hauāuru tribes
Te Huringa I (early)
wood, 38 cm long
OLD 13, Oldman collection, repatriated 1948.

119. Papahou (treasure box)
style of Tai Hauāuru tribes
Te Huringa I (early)
wood, 43 cm long
OLD 484, Oldman collection, repatriated 1948.

120. Wakahuia (treasure box)
style of Tai Rāwhiti tribes
Te Huringa I (middle)
wood, 66.5 cm long
OLD s3, Oldman collection, repatriated 1948

121. *Papahou* (treasure box)
style of Tai Tokerau tribes
Te Huringa I (early)
wood, 53.1 cm long
OLD 330, OLD 331, Oldman collection,
repatriated 1948
See figure 48.

122. *Papahou* (treasure box)
Te Huringa I (middle)
wood, 44 cm long
OLD 2, Oldman collection, repatriated

This box shows features of Tai Tokerau style. However, it was collected by Major-General Robley and is therefore more likely to have come from the Bay of Plenty.

123. *Papahou* (treasure box)
style of Tai Tokerau tribes
Te Huringa I (early)
wood, 38.8 cm long
WEB 864, Webster collection, repatriated 1958
See figure 39.

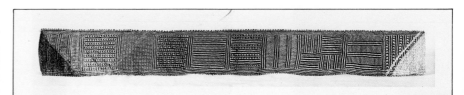

124. *Tauira* (samplers)
Ngāti Pikiao tribe of Te Arawa
Rotoiti
Te Huringa I (late)
Hamilton collection, acquired 1904
See figures 52 & 59.

These two samplers of *raranga* patterns used on *kete* (kits) were made for Augustus Hamilton by Te Hikapuhi of Ngāti Pikiao. Each pattern is named.

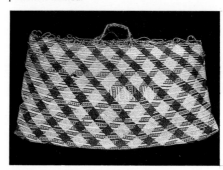

125. *Kete whakairo* (decorated kit)
Te Huringa I (early)
New Zealand flax, 60 cm wide, 28 cm high
ME 13967, repatriated 1977
See figure 57.

This kit was exhibited in London in 1833. It is not known when it was taken to England.

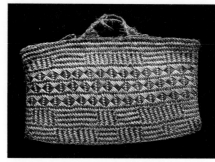

126. *Kete whakairo* (decorated kit)
Te Huringa I (late)
New Zealand flax, 41 cm wide, 28 cm high
ME 599, Hamilton collection, acquired 1904

When this kit was collected it was being used as a *pū kirikiri*, a kit for carrying sand.

Tauira) (sampler)
New Zealand flax, 327 cm long
ME 502

Tauira) (sampler)
New Zealand flax, 333 cm long
ME 503

127. *Kete whakairo* (decorated kit)
Tai Rāwhiti or Ngāti Kahungunu tribes
Te Huringa I (late)
New Zealand flax, 58 cm wide, 28 cm high
ME 296, Hill collection, acquired 1905

128. *Kete whakairo* (decorated kit)
Tai Rāwhiti or Ngāti Kahungunu tribes
Te Huringa I (late)
kiekie, New Zealand flax, 31 cm wide, 17 cm high
ME 297, Hill collection, acquired 1905

The kit is made of *kiekie*; the handles are of *muka* (prepared New Zealand flax fibre).

129. *Kete muka* (bag of dressed flax fibre)
Te Huringa I (late)
New Zealand flax, 30 cm wide, 26.5 cm high
ME 1776, acquired about 1905

130. *Kete muka* (bag of dressed flax fibre)
Te Huringa I (late)
New Zealand flax, 28.5 cm wide, 21 cm high
ME 11745, acquired 1967

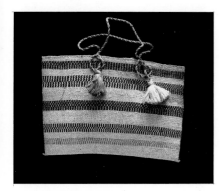

131. *Pūtea* (woven bag)
Ngāti Porou tribe
Te Huringa I (late)
New Zealand flax, 31 cm wide, 19.5 cm high
ME 1760, Tuta Nihoniho collection, acquired 1907

This bag and cat. no. 134 are part of a collection made by Tuta Nihoniho specially for the Museum in 1906 and 1907.

132. *Kete whakapuare* (open weave kit)
Te Huringa I (late)
New Zealand flax, 33 cm wide, 26 cm high
ME 11515

133. *Kete pīngao* (kit made from *pīngao*)
Tai Rāwhiti or Ngāti Kahungunu tribes
Te Huringa I (late)
pīngao, 37 cm wide, 21 cm high
ME 299, Hill collection, acquired 1905

134. *Kete tāniko* (woven bag)
Ngāti Porou tribe
Te Huringa I (late)
New Zealand flax, 35 cm wide, 18.5 cm high
ME 1765, Tuta Nihoniho collection, acquired 1907
See figure 58.

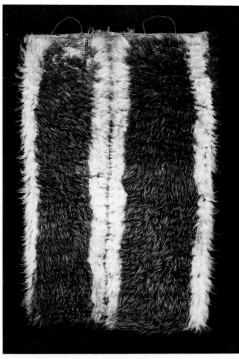

135. *Kahu-kiwi* (kiwi feather cloak)
Te Huringa I (middle)
New Zealand flax, kiwi feathers, 125 cm long,
155 cm wide
ME 1378, acquired about 1905
See figure 40.

136. *Kahu-kurī* (dog skin cloak)
Te Huringa I (early)
New Zealand flax, strips of haired dog skin,
124 cm long, 152 cm wide
ME 2052, Buller collection, acquired 1913

137. *Kahu-kurī* (dog skin cloak)
Te Huringa I (early)
New Zealand flax, strips of haired dog skin,
124 cm long, 141 cm wide
ME 2053, Buller collection, acquired 1913
See figure 23.

138. *Kahu-huruhuru* (feather cloak)
Te Huringa I (late)
New Zealand flax, feathers of kererū, tūī, kākā
and kākāriki; 119 cm long, 140 cm wide
ME 4275
See figure 2. (Inside front cover)

139. *Kahu-huruhuru* (feather cloak)
Te Huringa I (late)
New Zealand flax, feathers of kākā and tūī, 94 cm
long, 139 cm wide
ME 1773, acquired about 1909
See figure 56.

140. *Korowai* (tag cloak)
Te Huringa I (middle)
New Zealand flax, woollen yarn, 150 cm long,
179 cm wide
ME 14492, acquired 1985
This cloak was taken to England in the mid-nineteenth century.

141. *Kaitaka paepaeroa* (cloak with *tāniko* borders)
Ngāti Toa tribe
Te Huringa I (middle)
New Zealand flax, woollen yarn, 166 cm long,
215 cm wide
ME 14842, acquired 1986
see figure 53.

This cloak is said to have belonged to Tamihana Te Rauparaha, son of the fighting chief Te Rauparaha. Tamihana presented it to a Mr Christie, who took it to England. Christie's granddaughter returned it to New Zealand.

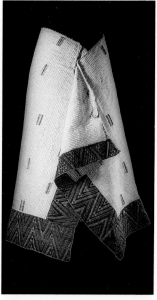

142. *Kaitaka paepaeroa* (cloak with *tāniko* borders)
Arawa tribes
Te Huringa I (late)
New Zealand flax, woollen yarn, 104 cm long,
178 cm wide
ME 11792, acquired 1967

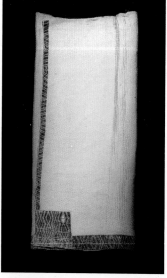

143. *Kaitaka paepaeroa* (cloak with *tāniko* borders)
Te Huringa I (early)
New Zealand flax, dog skin, woollen yarn, 137 cm
long, 165 cm wide
ME 13992, repatriated 1978
See figure 67 (Inside back cover)

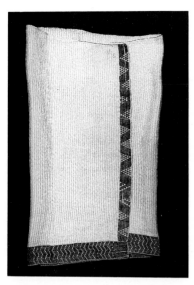

144. *Kaitaka paepaeroa* (cloak with *tāniko* borders)
Te Huringa I (early)
New Zealand flax, woollen yarn, 151 cm long,
210 cm wide
ME 13130, acquired 1974
(formerly Donne collection)

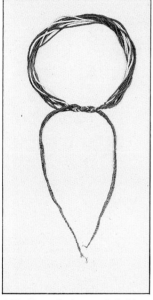

145. *Tū muka* (woman's belt)
Tūhoe tribe of Mataatua
Urewera
Te Huringa I (middle)
New Zealand flax, 205 cm long
ME 512, Hamilton collection, acquired 1904
The three colours were obtained by using undyed fibre, and fibre dyed with *hīnau* bark (red-brown) and *tānekaha* bark (black-brown).

146. *Tātua* (man's belt)
Te Huringa I (early)
New Zealand flax, haired dog skin, 287 cm long
ME 13966, repatriated 1977
(formerly Hooper collection)
This belt was presented to the Saffron Walden Museum in 1840 and acquired by Hooper in 1945.

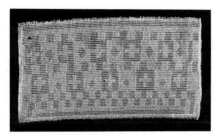

147. Altar frontal (?)
Te Huringa I (middle)
New Zealand flax, traces of feathers, 122 cm wide, 62 cm high
ME 13968, repatriated 1977
(formerly Hooper collection)

148. *Turuturu whatu* (weaving peg)
style of Tai Hauāuru tribes
Te Huringa I (middle)
wood, 49 cm high
ME 13842, Fletcher collection, acquired 1977
See figure 54.

149. *Turuturu whatu* (weaving peg)
Te Huringa I (early)
wood, 39.1 cm long'
OLD 157, Oldman collection, repatriated 1948

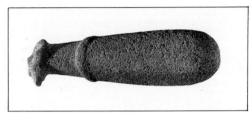

150. *Patu muka* (fibre beater)
Tai Hauāuru tribes
Te Huringa I (early)
andesite, 21.8 cm long
ME 1500, Donne collection, acquired 1905
Stone beaters are used in the preparation of *muka* (dressed fibre of New Zealand flax). Beaters with carved heads, as in this example, are largely confined to the Tai Hauāuru region.

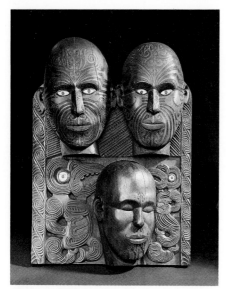

151. Carved panel
Ngāti Tarāwhai tribe of Te Arawa
Te Huringa I/II
wood, 77 cm high
ME 4211
See figure 63.

Tene Waitere of Ruato was commissioned by Augustus Hamilton in 1899 to carve this slab to illustrate facial tattoo. The oblique face was a departure from traditional practice.

153. *Kete muka*
Erenora Puketapu-Hetet
Te Ati Awa tribe
muka (prepared New Zealand flax fibre), 30.5 cm wide
ME 15025, acquired 1989
See figure 64.

The *kete* was woven in 1979. The techniques of *tāniko* and *whatu* were used and the fibre was dyed with traditional dyes.

155. "Manaia matau"
Warren Wilson
Te Ati Haunui-a-Paparangi tribe
nephrite, 7.5 cm high
ME 15020, acquired 1989

This small sculpture is based on traditional fishhook shapes.

152. "Kōkiri — the wall hanging"
Erenora Puketapu-Hetet
Te Ati Awa tribe
muka (prepared New Zealand flax fibre) and feathers of pheasant, pūkeko and duck, 96 cm high
ME 15024, acquired 1989

Kōkiri — the wall hanging was woven in 1981 and reflects the Kōkiri policy of the Maori Affairs Department in the late 1970s which encouraged the Maori people to advance on a number of fronts. It has been woven in the traditional way, with the traditional materials presented in a contemporary manner.

154. Pendant
Hepi Maxwell
Ngāti Rangiwewehi tribe of Te Arawa
nephrite, 6 cm long
ME 15019, acquired 1989
See figure 61.

The traditional spiral of carving and *kōwhaiwhai* is the basis for the design of this pendant.

156. "Ngā whānau a Māhu"
Emmitt Aranga
Ngāi Tūhoe tribe
whalebone, 12.2 cm long
ME 15021, acquired 1989
See figure 60.

This pendant reflects the Tūhoe story of Māhu and his brother-in-law Taewha.

157. "Hei matau"

Moanaroa Zagrobelna
Te Whānau-a-Apanui and Te Ati Awa tribes
whale ivory, 5.4 cm long
ME 15022, acquired 1989
See figure 65.

The nephrite *hei matau* in the Te Maori exhibition was the inspiration for this pendant.

158. "Manawa rere kitea"

Moanaroa Zagrobelna
Te Whānau-a-Apanui and Te Ati Awa tribes
whale ivory, 7.7 cm long
ME 15023, acquired 1989

Manawa rere kitea can be translated as "My heart soared heavenward when I first saw you". The artist bases many of her designs on the bush and sea. The *koru* (fern frond) motif can be seen in this pendant.

159. "He purapura i ruia mai i Rangiātea"

Robyn Kahukiwa
Ngāti Porou tribe
Oil on unstretched canvass, 1985
1339 x 1027 mm
Collection of National Art Gallery, New Zealand

The title, which can be translated as "The seed scattered abroad from Rangiātea", refers to the same concept as that used by Mead to characterise the earliest style period of Maori Art as *Ngā Kākano* (the seeds). The *poutokomanawa* figures from the centre posts of carved houses are here depicted in a different medium.

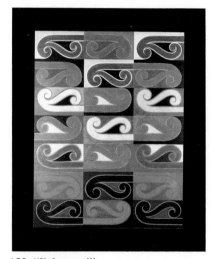

160. "Kahurangi"

Sandy Adsett
Ngāti Kahungunu
Acrylic on board, 1988
1265 x 1070 mm
Collection of National Art Gallery, New Zealand
See figure 66.

The artist explains: Kahurangi is a *koiri* unit arrangement of the *koru* symbol in a free order pattern. It is an acknowledgement of, and pays respect to, the traditional base of the geometric discipline of *kōwhaiwhai*.

161. "Ngā kete o te Wānanga"

Jim Wiki
Te Aupouri
Oamaru stone, 75 cm tall, 1989
ME 15027, acquired 1989

The carving represents the ascent of Tānenuiārangi to the top of the twelfth heaven to obtain the three ancestral kits of knowledge.

162. _Poupou_
Mauriora Kingi
Tuhourangi of Te Arawa and Ngāti Raukawa
wood, 277 cm high
ME 15026, acquired 1989

This carving depicts Tamatekapua, captain of the Arawa canoe (above) and his younger brother Whakaturia (below). Using stilts, they stole breadfruit from the garden of a chief in Hawaiki. They later migrated to Aotearoa (New Zealand) from Hawaiki.

163. _Poupou_
Roi Toia
Ngā Puhi tribe
wood, 195 cm high
ME 15028, acquired 1989

The carving illustrates a traditional story explaining the origin of various fish. The figures are Tangaroa and Kiwa.